ADHD 2.0 EFFECT ON MARRIAGE

Target 7 Days

Margaret Hampton

ADHD 2.0 EFFECT ON MARRIAGE

Target 7 Days

Turn Anger into Love
Overcome Anxiety in Relationship | Couple Conflicts |
Insecurity in Love
Improve Communication Skills | Empath & Psychic Abilities

Margaret Hampton

Contents

Introduction

Are you in a marriage that sometimes feels more like a relationship between a parent and a child? Do you feel like one of you is taking on a larger burden of care and it's straining your partnership? Is one or both of you forgetful or disorganized to the point of dysfunction? Does your house always feel like a reflection of the mess that is your life?

If all this feels almost painfully familiar, you may be in an ADHD-affected relationship. ADHD affects somewhere between 4 and 6 percent of adults and it's been found that ADHD-affected marriages end in divorce at nearly twice the rate of non-affected marriages. That doesn't mean there's no hope for you and your partner, though. It can seem intimidating to tackle a problem that feels so large and leaves you both feeling like everything is out of control. This book is designed to help you understand more about the disorder and how it affects relationships. We're going to take you through seven days of work to get your marriage back on track, help eliminate the insecurities and anxieties that stem from the disorder, and build your love and empathy for each other back to where it was when you first fell in love.

We'll start by learning more about what ADHD is and isn't, and what traits of ADHD are affecting your marriage. This book aims to help both the affected and non-affected spouses. You can work together or you can apply the techniques and tips you've learned on your own.

Day One will look at turning your frustration around. It could feel overwhelming being constantly upset at the things that your spouse does. You blame them or blame yourself for the issues in your relationship, but you can learn to turn those negative feelings back into feelings of love and compassion.

Day Two will help you overcome the anxieties that crop up in relationships with ADHD. Sometimes it can seem like the disorder turns our partner into the Incredible Hulk. They can be quick to anger or quick to respond with strong emotion, which can leave you feeling confused and upset. Other times feel like they're ignoring you to focus on something that seems insignificant to you. Are they spending hours and hours on their hobbies or interests? You'll learn how to understand them better and how to fix things when you feel the distance growing.

Day Three will look at how the disorder can affect people's ability to form secure attachments and how they may struggle with the social skills necessary for a successful relationship. You'll learn how to help your affected spouse with their relationship skills and better understand each other's nonverbal cues. We will also include tips for couples who struggle with interpersonal relationships outside the home and how to navigate those situations as a couple.

Day Four will have you learning more about the conflict that arises in relationships with an affected partner and how to manage conflict within the relationship. Sometimes the disorder can affect how you deal with conflict in the relationship. You'll learn how to become more comfortable with conflict when necessary and become a better listener and a better problem solver.

Day Five will be all about improving your communication skills. Sometimes within an ADHD-affected marriage, it can be difficult for the non-affected spouse to get their point across to the ADHD-affected spouse. We'll look at some solutions to common communication issues and when to seek outside help for the relationship.

Day Six will focus on how to eliminate the insecurities in your relationships. In addition, we will delve into ways to improve the affected spouse's self-esteem and build confidence in the relationship, and how to communicate constructive feedback effectively.

Day Seven will be all about fostering empathy and love for each other. You'll learn how to become more empathetic, and ways to fall in love all over again after the issues around the disorder have strained your relationship. You'll also learn about your affected partner's qualities that can actually make your marriage better and how to nurture those qualities in your spouse.

When learning about how the disorder affects your marriage, the first step is to understand more about ADHD and what it is. Attention Deficit/Hyperactive Disorder is a neurological disorder that has no defined cause as of yet. It's thought to be caused by a combination of factors such as environment, genetics, and fetal development. It's most often thought of as a disorder that affects young boys, but there are still a significant number of girls and women affected by ADHD. Unfortunately, for various reasons, the disorder goes underdiagnosed in women to this day.

It is a spectrum disorder, and there are three primary types: Hyperactive-Impulsive, Inattentive, and Combination. Boys are more likely to be diagnosed with Hyperactive-Impulsive while girls are more likely to be diagnosed with Inattentive type ADHD. Both genders can experience any of the three types, though.

Some of the symptoms include:

- Impulsive behaviors
- Poor time management skills
- Issues focusing on a task
- Trouble with multitasking
- Disorganization and problems prioritizing
- Frequent moods swings
- Low tolerance for external stimuli
- Low tolerance for frustration
- Restlessness or excessive energy

- Inability to sit still
- Difficulty coping with stress
- Emotional dysregulation
- Short attention span
- Appearing forgetful or frequently losing things
- Being easily distracted
- Poor organization

It can feel frustrating to deal with a spouse who seems to have the attention span of a goldfish. You feel like you're constantly repeating information you think they should remember. You might be experiencing frustration with their impulsive behaviors or even get upset when their impulses lead them to make decisions such as financing a new car when there's a baby on the way. It can feel like their inability to stay organized means you have to carry the load of the household duties, lest nothing gets done.

These are all common symptoms of the disorder. They can be managed with things like medication, therapy, and exercise. Even if they are not properly managed, there are ways that you, as the non-affected spouse, can help your affected spouse cope with the difficulties that the disorder brings. The two of you can work together to create a better, more fulfilling relationship!

We have seven days to turn things around. So let's start with day one.

Day 1

Turn Frustration Into Love

Exercise: Sit together in a neutral space, such as the living room or on the porch. Avoid doing this in intimate spaces like the bedroom or personal spaces like your home office. Light a candle. Each of you will then take turns making "I feel" statements to each other about your current frustrations, such as "I feel frustrated that I'm doing most of the cooking lately and it's getting tiring for me." Acknowledge each other's feelings. Don't agree or disagree; just acknowledge how your partner feels at that moment.

After letting out your feelings, blow out the candle. The candle will symbolize releasing your frustrations and letting go of anger. You can now talk through your "I feel" statements if you want, but during the exercise, the point is to give each other space to listen and feel heard.

The disorder comes with a host of symptoms that, believe it or not, can directly affect your ability to navigate relationships healthily. In addition, symptoms can cause misunderstandings, frustration, and resentment on the part of either partner. These symptoms can be difficult to deal with in everyday life but can be damaging in a relationship.

When you're a person with ADHD, it might feel like your partner is hypercritical or constantly nagging you about your household chores. You don't feel respected or treated as an equal; you even start to feel as though you're being treated like a child. It can feel like your significant other wants to micromanage you, and you start to wonder if the relationship is worth the struggles. You feel frustrated that nothing you do seems to be right. No matter what, you feel like you're constantly making mistakes or doing things the wrong way.

Being constantly berated by your spouse might bring up bad childhood memories—memories of being bullied or looked down on for being different. Maybe you went into this marriage thinking you finally met someone who understands you and accepts you, but now you're questioning if that's still true. People with this disorder are often more sensitive to criticism, especially if they feel like they've been criticized their entire lives for not being "normal" enough. This is definitely something that can lead to insecurities building up over time. You wonder if your spouse thinks you're good enough, and it might wear on your self-esteem.

For the non-affected spouse, you feel ignored when you make requests. You get lonely when your spouse gets hyper-fixated on a project or frustrated at the amount of time they spend on their hobby, leading to resentment from feeling neglected and like you're carrying more of the emotional labor. You might also be getting upset when you feel like you're the only reliable partner in the relationship. It can get exhausting wondering if they will follow through on their promises. It can start to feel like they just don't care.

It could be extremely tough if you went into the marriage with expectations that your partner would get better. No one should go into a marriage expecting their partner to change, but it happens. You might have believed that once the affected spouse "settled down," they would take adult responsibilities more seriously, especially when children become involved in the equation.

These frustrations can be understandable. Dealing with them is probably exhausting for both partners. It's easy to blame the affected spouse. Still, with a deeper understanding of how the disorder works and the common problems that can arise in a relationship with someone affected by the disorder, you will be able to eliminate those frustrations. Let's go over the symptoms of ADHD again, specifically the ones that most affect relationships:

- **Trouble paying attention**: Having this disorder might mean you zone out during conversations, miss important details, or agree to something you later forget about. You feel like you're trying to pay attention but you can easily become distracted in a busy environment. You aren't trying to ignore your partner or forget what they said, but it might feel that way to them. You feel as though you have tried to explain this but it can be frustrating to someone who is neurotypical because they may not fully understand how difficult it can be.

- **Forgetfulness**: It can feel like even when your partner *is* paying attention, they end up forgetting what was discussed anyway. It might seem like the only important things to *them* are those they remember, but that's not true. ADHD brains can store long-term memories without issue but struggle with retaining short-term memories. That's why they might be able to recite pi to the one-hundredth digit but can't seem to remember to pick up cat litter on the way home from work.

- **Emotional outbursts**; People with ADHD have a harder time with emotional regulation. Their brains can't properly process emotional responses and strong emotions can overwhelm them until they're bursting. For people with this disorder, it can feel like your body gets hot when you're angry or upset, and for your partner, it may feel like they are walking on eggshells to keep from upsetting you.

- **Poor organizational skills**: Having the disorder is like a constant whirlwind in your head. It can be hard to keep track of your own thoughts, let alone all the tasks necessary to keep a household going. It may feel like the affected spouse is just lazy or disorganized, but in reality, there's a lot more going on. It can certainly be frustrating though, to feel like the majority of household tasks fall to you. The ADHD-affected partner may feel frustrated and guilty at the way their partner feels and lash out as a defense.

3

- **Impulsivity**: ADHD-related impulsivity can be a struggle. Sometimes you have no brain-to-mouth filter. You end up thoughtlessly blurting out something hurtful without realizing it. Your brain craves the rush of dopamine that comes from instant gratification and wants you to spend recklessly or you crave addictive behaviors. This can affect your relationship with your partner in many ways, from financial stress to your spouse feeling that you put your addictions above your family.

The first step to overcoming some of the frustrations that come from dealing with this disorder, either as the affected partner or the neurotypical partner, is to understand how each of you is feeling when dealing with these issues. Are you stressed carrying the majority of the household duties? Do you feel like you're juggling a dozen plates in the air at all times and if you let one plate drop, the entire thing will come crashing down? Do you feel like you can't rely on your affected partner and they are adding to your stress?

You probably try to give your partner advice. You offer solutions. You send them reminders. Nothing seems to work. You feel like they are ignoring you on purpose. When you need encouragement or a positive compliment, you feel like that seems always to be the moment your partner blurts out something rude or off-putting. You feel like they go out of their way to hit you where it hurts during your arguments. It can feel like they are going out of their way to upset you.

Carrying the emotional load can be hard. You might be at your wit's end, feeling as if nothing you do is getting through to your partner, as if nothing will ever change. That can be an exhausting experience. As you struggle with the issues caused by the disorder, it can feel like your ability to desire and love your partner is waning. It might feel like you don't know how to connect emotionally anymore. When your affected partner chooses to engage for hours on a hyper fixation or spends weeks or months of their free time focused on a project instead of connecting with you, you can start to question their loyalty and devotion. No matter how much you beg, plead, threaten, cajole, discuss or yell, nothing changes. You even start to feel like you're on the verge of a breakdown.

It can be hard on the non-affected spouse, for sure. However, it can often be just as difficult for the affected partner. They have their own emotional turmoil. It can feel like you are the only one feeling frustrated, but the problems are a two-way street.

ADHD can be a stressful disorder. You're sensitive to many kinds of stimuli whether that be noises, textures, foods, or smells. It can be overwhelming trying to process throughout the day. Managing daily life can also be much more work than others realize. People with this disorder often experience the world uniquely, which others may not understand. You feel like you're almost speaking a different language to your partner, trying to explain how things work for you. It can feel like you'll never live up to others' expectations. You feel like you're constantly making mistakes or failing at things you set out to do. You could be overcompensating with humor or lashing out in anger to hide your true feelings. When bombarded by criticisms from your partner, your boss, family, and friends, you can start to feel like people don't care about you, just the person they want you to be. You feel like your failure to live up to expectations pushes your partner away. You can start to feel like they don't want you around and rebuff your attempts at connection. The more times you fail to meet expectations, the more fear you have of the consequences. You become too afraid even to try anymore. One of the strongest desires for people with ADHD is to be accepted. You might be longing for your partner to love you for who you are despite your imperfections.

There are many ways symptoms can affect your relationships, but these are the most common areas likely to give you trouble and cause a significant strain. The frustrations may have built up to the point where you and your partner feel a divide that can't be bridged. It doesn't have to stay like that, however. Medication and therapy are good ways to help. There are also ways to cross that divide with techniques that you can use together, right at home. Here are a few techniques to help you and your partner avoid or overcome some of the problems that arise with ADHD:

For the non-affected partner

When you're getting stressed out by your spouse's actions, you're more likely to lash out at them. All the nagging and verbal confrontations in the world haven't helped so far and will continue to make your spouse feel more defensive than helped. Time to learn to let go and know you can only control yourself. Use positive reinforcement with them. It might feel unnecessary or condescending but saying something like, "Hey, thanks for taking the trash out today! I meant to ask, but you beat me to it!" goes a long way towards positively reinforcing the behavior you want to see. Acknowledge their efforts and achievements. Letting them know you're proud of them for sticking with a new routine or habit can also help them in the long run.

On the other hand, don't go so far as to act like their parent. It can feel like nagging your partner is what works, but treating them as a child or being condescending can damage your relationship and destroy their self-esteem. Communicate the issue and then let them deal with the consequences if they are unable or unwilling to follow through. Don't take over their duties either. You'll only grow in your resentment the more you take on. Try to focus on their intentions instead of their shortcomings. It may feel like they're ignoring you when they lose concentration but remember, it's not about you; it's their brain. You feel as though your partner finds you uninteresting, but they likely don't mean to make you feel unloved.

For the affected partner

Start by acknowledging what's happening. Your partner might not be communicating in a way that you like, but the fact is, your issues *are* interfering in your relationship. You need to acknowledge that the problem isn't solely on your partner to fix you and your issues, that it's on you as well. You are a team, and you can't expect your partner to act as your manager. If you know that a conversation is turning into an argument or that a situation provokes strong emotions in you, have an agreed-upon code word that you two use when things are getting out of your control. Use the code word to signal to your partner that you two need to take a break from the conversation or situation until you can calm down and regroup. Pick something that wouldn't come up in everyday conversation, such as "Kumquat" or "Ollivander."

When your spouse feels cared for, even with small gestures, that can go a long way towards making them feel more valued. When they go out of their way to take care of an issue you've been struggling with, don't get upset! Show them gratitude and understand that they're only trying to help. You know you have ADHD. Are you utilizing all the help and resources to manage your condition? Are you exploring treatment options and looking up ways to help yourself in your weak spots? If you don't have a toolbox of tools to use, you're not being fair to your partner. Once you start learning to manage the symptoms that make life more difficult for you and your partner, life will become smoother.

The two of you should work together to pick ways to mitigate stress. Do things like having a no-chores day. Yes, it's important to keep up with the housework, but it can sometimes feel like a lot of your problems revolve around the division of labor or who is and isn't doing their fair share. Pick one day a week that you both agree on that remains a chore-free day. It might feel stressful at first to let go, but you should both focus on quality time or enjoy free time to do things you might not normally get to do. Whether that's simply binge-watching a show together or spending time on your hobbies in the same room, do something that you enjoy and doesn't revolve around responsibility.

Sometimes when the two of you are having a conflict or disagreement and tensions are high, you can feel like you're simply angry or frustrated. Take a step back to identify the heart of the emotion. There's a saying that there are only two emotions: love and fear. This is simplistic, but, when it comes down to it, maybe as the non-affected partner, you fear that your partner will never step up and you'll be alone in the relationship. Perhaps as the affected partner, you fear your partner getting fed up and leaving you. You're both coming from the same place—the fear of being alone. Real love isn't a feeling so much as it's an action. It can be difficult to choose your partner day in and day out, especially when they're driving you to frustration, but you picked that person for a reason. Take a few minutes out of your day, both of you, to sit and list five things you like about your partner. You don't have to say them out loud to each other (though that can be helpful), but it will help you remember that there are qualities you love about them.

Of course, sometimes, it can get to the point where it feels like nothing is changing. Maybe you are in a rut, and an outside opinion can help. There are many options—everything from seeing your spiritual advisor if you belong to a religious group to going to a licensed family counselor. If cost is an issue, there are many free or sliding-scale options out there. You both need to go into the session with open minds and let go of the idea that the blame rests solely on one person. When trying to turn the relationship around and improve your conflict-resolution skills, it can help to step back and put yourself in your partner's shoes. Think about the way your partner might feel in reaction to your statements. Think through how they might be feeling about the situation. You can gain a lot of clarity if you take that time to recognize and acknowledge their perspective.

You and your partner might be spending a lot of time misinterpreting each other's actions and intentions. When you're disagreeing, you could be assigned your interpretation to what you're hearing without giving your partner the benefit of the doubt. For example, when the non-ADHD affected partner says, "When you spend all day working on the car, I feel like I have to take care of the kids by myself," this may come across as accusations of being lazy to the affected partner. Instead, practice active listening. When your partner makes a statement, repeat your understanding of their words. This will allow them to clarify their intent and meaning.

When dealing with this disorder, there's one really great way to approach any problem that arises. For those affected, it may be difficult to do things the "normal" or "usual" way, and you need to adapt and change your approach, finding what works. If it feels stupid, but it works, it's not stupid. For the non-affected partner, you're going to have to get past the idea that your partner "should" do things a certain way, or you're going to drive a wedge trying to make the affected spouse live up to your expectations.

Don't forget to lean into the unconventional and find humor in dealing with the situation. Sometimes, you have to laugh at just how absurd life with a chronic condition can be. Learning to laugh at the silly miscommunications and the wild misunderstandings can help you both relieve some of the tension and even bring you closer together. When you

8

get the urge to impulsively say something negative, use an imaginary key or mime zipping your mouth up so you don't blurt out something hurtful. When tensions are high or stress is piling up, take time out of your schedules to work out. Take a walk, do yoga, or have a mini dance party. Get up and moving as exercise gives you endorphins that can help combat stress and fatigue. It also has a positive effect on ADHD, helping to calm the brain and improve focus.

If communicating face-to-face is difficult or causes strong emotional reactions, write down the things you want to say to each other via email. It gives you the space to sort out your feelings and can be a good way to express the things you have a hard time saying. Alternatively, send each other kind and loving emails once a day or once a week to remind each other how much you care. It doesn't need to be long, but it should be thoughtful. Also, getting educated on ADHD and its symptoms and difficulties means understanding how it's affecting your relationship. It's good for both partners–the affected partner might learn new techniques that help manage their symptoms and make life easier, and the non-affected spouse might be able to take the challenges less seriously. Check in once a week with each other to have the opportunity to discuss any issues and celebrate the progress you two have made. Use it as an opportunity to grow as a couple. Lastly, sometimes you have to give up on the idea that it should always fall to the two of you to take care of everything. Instead, outsource help or delegate tasks. For example, get groceries delivered, assign your children age-appropriate chores and set up automatic drafts for bills. These will eliminate a lot of the worries and stresses that you face.

It will take work to move from daily frustrations back to love and empathy. There are going to be missteps along the way. You may feel like it's two steps forward and one step back some days. It's okay to be frustrated. It's okay to feel your feelings. It's not about achieving perfect harmony, total balance, and complete serenity. It's about finding ways to work with the tools you have to create the lives you want for yourselves. When you use your tools, you're less likely to feel as though you can't do it–you know you're empowered enough to get it done. You don't have to be perfect; you just have to learn how to embrace your imperfections. With ADHD, you have hyperfocus–this can help you in so many ways.

The best way to start is to create an action plan. Come up with a way that the two of you will work together; using the tips above to make a change for the better. When you have a plan in place, you have something to fall back on when things repeatedly start to slip out of control. For example, you struggle with setting up organizational systems. Your partner can step in here and offer assistance with coming up with ideas that work for both of you. Remember, if it's stupid, but it works, it's not stupid.

Start by analyzing the areas in which you two have the most conflict. Do you struggle with your partner remembering to do the things that you ask? Is your partner chronically late? Does the division of labor feel unfair? Next, come up with practical, actionable solutions. For things like forgotten requests, stick a post-it note inside your partner's lunchbox, text them a reminder before they leave work, or write them on a dry erase board by the door. For chronic lateness, set up calendar reminders that you can share across your phones, set timers for yourself if you know you underestimate how much time you have, and make sure you work backward on timing–add in everything from getting ready to walking out the door to finding parking.

If chores are going undone, develop a routine. Having a daily routine in place will help you both to remember what needs to get done that day. Start with the morning and work your way through to the evening, developing a list of what you do all day. For instance, you usually wake up at eight, then eat breakfast, brush your teeth, get dressed, and feed the dog. Writing it down will help you remember so you don't have to mentally remember it. It may seem silly, but you'll associate each step with the next one by writing all the steps down. You'll be less likely to forget to brush your teeth if you know you do it after eating breakfast. You'll remember to feed the dog because that comes directly after brushing your teeth.

Additionally, set up a system for controlling the clutter in the house. Less clutter means less anxiety which means less avoidance of tasks. Get baskets for the stairs or the living room where you put all the stuff that doesn't go there. Drop it in the basket, and when it's full, clear it out by putting things away. Do the dishes immediately after dinner instead of waiting so you aren't as likely to put it off. After eating breakfast, put the dishes away in the drainer first so they don't sit there all day. Come up with ways that work with your ADHD, and you'll be less likely to be overwhelmed by the amount of mess or clutter around you.

When it comes to remembering questions, repeat what your partner said and what you agreed to do. That ensures that you both know you were listening and are more likely to remember the task the way it was intended. Write it down on a post-it, in your planner or as a note on your phone so that you don't forget either. Set a reminder using an app on your phone to go off when it's time to do the task or remind you of the task if you start to get busy and are likely to forget it. Setting a reminder will draw you out of your hyperfocused state as well, so you don't spend too long on any one activity.

With a plan in place, you'll both feel more equipped to take on missteps as they happen. Of course, you probably won't always get it right, but things will run much more smoothly than they have been. Navigating the difficulties of the disorder can feel like a game of chance, but by using these tips and techniques, life is guaranteed to be much less stressful for you both.

When you've started to notice a change in the way things are running, you might be ready to spend more time together reconnecting and building intimacy. The non-affected partner will feel less burdened and less like a parent to the ADHD-affected partner. The affected partner will feel like they are accepted and wanted by the person they married. It's a win for everyone involved.

Chapter Summary

- ADHD symptoms can affect your relationship in many ways. Some of the most common symptoms that affect the relationship involve struggles with time management, organization, impulsive behavior, and emotional dysregulation.

- Both of you have a lot of feelings and emotions that the other might not understand or be aware of. It will help to take a step back and express how you're both feeling to better understand what the other is going through.

- For the non-affected spouse, remember to be patient, focus on their intentions, use positive reinforcement, and stop acting like their parent.

- For the affected spouse, it's important to acknowledge your role in the situation, take a step back when emotions run high, and build your resource toolbox for managing your symptoms.

- For both of you, remember to identify your emotions, set aside time for each other or just relax, put yourself in the other's shoes and go to counseling to help you talk through things you're still struggling with.

- There are a lot of unconventional ways you can work through your issues as well, such as participating in exercise together, finding humor in the absurd, and educating yourself more about ADHD.

- Put a plan in place for how you're going to improve things moving forward. Outsource and delegate tasks to lighten the load, act as a team and set up reminders, schedule weekly check-ins to see how things are going, and discuss concerns and develop a daily routine to help things run more smoothly.

In the next chapter, we're going to discuss overcoming anxieties in the relationship. We'll take a closer look at the ways you and your partner might be feeling distant from each other and how to bridge that gap.

Day 2

Overcome Relationship Anxieties

Exercise: Pick a room where you spend a lot of time together, like the bedroom. Sit together, facing each other. Take ten deep breaths, in for four, hold for four, out for six.

Reach out and hold each other's hands. Close your eyes and focus on the sensation of what you're feeling. Focus on the way you feel connected through your hands. Focus until the only thing you're aware of is the sound of their breathing and the feeling of their skin on yours.

Move your hands to each part of your partner's body in turn. Start with their hands and move in this order: hands, arms, shoulders, face, hair, chest, abdomen, thighs, lower legs, feet, back up to the thighs, and then optionally, onto your partner's sexual organs. Continue to meditate on each part in turn.

The purpose of this exercise is to feel more deeply connected and attuned to each other's bodies.

ADHD definitely affects your partner regarding relationship anxieties, but how do you experience anxiety? People with this disorder are more likely to suffer from comorbidities like depression, anxiety, and disordered behavior than their neurotypical counterparts. Anxiety can be a built-in part of the experience for many. It can feel all-consuming, with intrusive thoughts that plague you about the future and your lives together. Fear of the unknown can make you act rashly or badly in situations where understanding is needed.

Relationship anxieties are usually related to past experiences and trauma and, left unchecked, can poison even the healthiest of partnerships. Anxiety is like a wound that, left untreated, can end up destroying the body. Some of the worst anxieties that affected people face can add to the stress of relationships. For example, your partner may have impulsive behaviors that lead you to worry about the state of your finances. Impulsive behaviors and addictive tendencies are common. Your partner may be addicted to playing video games, spending too much money, or even having a more serious addiction to drugs or alcohol. It can be worrisome when they have an addictive personality, wondering what to do about their addiction and how to cope. You might also be feeling like you come second to your partner's special interests, and you feel like your partner doesn't listen when you tell them about your day or how you're feeling.

The difficulties with inattention might be making you feel ignored. Suppose your partner is constantly forgetting the things you say or forgetting important anniversaries, or not stepping up and showing their appreciation in ways that are meaningful to you. In that case, you might even start to wonder if they care. You could also feel like your partner expects you to perfectly manage them and their symptoms—that you need to be the "strong" one, the one in complete control who reminds them what they forgot or helps them when they have strong ADHD-powered emotions. You feel stressed at the thought that you're not always capable of meeting those needs.

For the affected partner, it can be all the same anxieties as the non-affected spouse and more. You probably spend a lot of time stressing about the future and what might happen instead of allowing yourself to be present and in the present in the relationship. People with ADHD often rush into relationships, craving the high of new love and then worrying about being "good enough" to sustain it. Additionally, you may experience a lot of anxiety revolving around your own negative qualities and how they're affecting the relationship. Due to a combination of poor self-esteem and past trauma, you could be assuming that a breakup is inevitable. You analyze every interaction and pick it apart for signs.

For people with the disorder, you could have had unfulfilling or bad past relationships, and you worry that the same problems will crop up again. You obsess over not repeating those mistakes, or you feel like you can't get a handle on the issues that led to the demise of your current relationship. Being socially adept is challenging for anyone but especially for people with this disorder. It might be stressful trying to decipher your partner's body language and decide whether or not they're upset with you. You are stressed about inadvertently or unintentionally embarrassing your partner in social situations. It can feel like you have to be careful about everything you say and do, especially if you had an overbearing parent about your social shortcomings.

When something goes wrong, you or your partner may place a lot of the blame on your symptoms. This can lead to you stressing over the idea that the relationship issues are your fault. You internalize the message. Instead of thinking, "this is from one of my symptoms," you tell yourself, "I am a terrible person causing issues."

Of course, this is just a snapshot of the types of anxieties that each spouse may be facing. The list is endless. Anxiety, like depression, likes to feed off of itself to remain a constant in the life of its host. The two of you may not even realize how many anxieties you have in common. Sharing those anxieties is the first step to overcoming them. Here are some ways you can better manage anxiety in relationships:

1. Practice mindfulness. Mindfulness is learning to be fully present and aware of what you're feeling and experiencing and doing in a non-judgmental, accepting way. There are many ways to practice mindfulness, from checking in with yourself every few hours to using meditation to center yourself and focus on your thoughts and feelings. Both of you need to spend time centering yourself and understanding what you're feeling, where you're feeling it in your body, and why you feel the way you do. Mindfulness can help with that. As you become more aware of your feelings, you'll know how to combat negative thoughts.

2. Practice breathing. When you're feeling anxious or panicky or upset, taking a moment to breathe can make all the difference. Try different breathing techniques for calming yourself and bringing yourself back to a neutral state. Taking a step away during a disagreement to focus on your breathing can also be helpful, not only to quell anxieties but to re-center yourself.

3. Challenge your fear. Whenever a fear or anxiety crops up, face it head-on. Explain to yourself why the fear is unfounded. If you worry your partner will leave you, look at your wedding photos to remind yourself that they're committed to you for better or worse. If you fear that the house will never get spotless, remind yourself that it doesn't have to be perfect, just clean *enough*. A little dust on the baseboards never killed anyone. You can always sit down and discuss your fears with your partner as well. Your partner may be more reassuring than you expect and less judgmental than you fear.

4. Identify your triggers. If certain things or situations trigger your anxieties, identify those. You can help your spouse by avoiding those things that upset them or finding ways to help them when those pop up. For example, if new social situations trigger your spouse's ADHD, stick with them to help them navigate a new situation. Leaving them to fend for themselves isn't fair or kind. As the non-ADHD spouse, if you are highly bothered by clothes all over the bedroom floor, set a timer for 15 minutes where the two of you clean up all the clothes, putting them away or in the laundry. Working together can help you both feel more like a team.

5. Practice socializing. It can be incredibly stressful to navigate social situations, especially for people with ADHD. Practice socializing either with your spouse or a counselor. You can go over situations and how to handle them and any kind of issues that crop up for you. For example, maybe you talk over people too much while socializing. Practice using small cues like a tap on the wrist with your spouse that they can use when you're dominating the conversation. You'll feel more confident that you can enjoy social situations without being off-putting.

6. Have a safeword. Sometimes when things get overwhelming, you just need an out. Use a safeword like "sunshine" or "Carole Baskin" to let your spouse know that you're experiencing anxiety in a situation. It

17

doesn't matter if you're around other people or you're using it in private, using your safeword should mean that your spouse knows you need comforting. The non-affected spouse should aim to make the affected spouse as comfortable as possible, either removing them from the situation or ending the discussion until further notice.

7. Commit to commitment. As people affected, we often crave excitement and new situations. This can easily lead to feeling the urge to stray. When this happens, you should talk to your spouse, first and foremost, and definitely seek therapy. In addition to that, find ways to spice things up with your spouse. Pick something exciting to look forward to doing together. This can be as simple as a new movie you both want to see or as wild as trying new sexual positions on an exotic vacation. The important thing is to focus on staying committed to your spouse.

8. Forgive and forget. Holding grudges or holding onto all the ways you two have messed up over the years is not only toxic for your relationship, but it can easily destroy your self-esteem. Learn to let go of your anger and frustration and forgive your partner for their mistakes. You also have to learn to let it go and no longer bring up past transgressions. It will be much healthier in the long run. You're spending a lifetime together, petty grudges have no place here.

9. Only one crazy person in the house at a time. Make it a rule that when one of you is freaking out or having a panic attack, the other has to be calm and collected. Only one person is allowed to go nuts at any given time. It's a silly but effective rule.

10. Find ways to connect. When you have anxieties over the state of the relationship, take time to connect. Play a video game together, pick a tv show to binge-watch on your favorite streaming service, or do an activity together like taking a walk or completing a puzzle. The simple act of doing something together will be reassuring and comforting. You'll feel more connected to each other when you spend quality time together. It can be hard to find the time in this busy world but schedule it out if needed. Set aside one hour a week where the two of you sit down or get out and do something together.

11. Seek help. Sometimes you need more help than a few breathing exercises can provide. Whether you go to a counselor or see your healthcare provider for medication, find a way to manage the anxiety that works for you. There's no shame in needing the extra help. Sometimes, fighting depression and anxiety can feel like fighting a war. You can't win a war if you're not properly prepared. Medication can be like the armor that protects you during battle. It's armor that you can use to get through. However, you can't win a war without proper assistance. You need fellow soldiers and leaders who can guide you through. Mental health specialists can be like your leaders, while your friends and family can be your fellow fighters. Once properly prepared to fight, there's no way you can lose.

Anxiety can easily get the best of us. Sometimes, it can get so bad that it destroys the relationship. When this happens, you need to take a serious step back and reach for help. Some of the most damaging behaviors to relationships stem from anxiety. Be on the lookout for behaviors that show that your partner lets their anxieties control them in damaging ways. Your partner has the right to a certain degree of say in a relationship, but you also have a right to decide what that level of control looks like. It's an issue when they begin to decide things for you that you don't agree with or feel uncomfortable about. Anxiety can drive people to control their partner's actions in fear of what might happen to them if they don't take control. This is unfair and infantilizing to your adult spouse. Try to realize that your partner is their own person with their own mind, and they deserve to be treated like an adult. Being constantly interrogated about where you're going or who you're with can feel stifling. Does your partner accuse you of things baselessly? Be aware of this red flag. Your partner might be coming from a place of anxiety and poor self-esteem, maybe feeling like they're in a relationship with someone "out of their league" or "too good for them," but ultimately, that's a problem for them to fix. Try to nip it in the bud as quickly as possible when this crops up.

Jealousy can stem from a multitude of places that are all rooted in insecurity and anxiety. It's easy to get swallowed up by the green-eyed monster when you feel like your spouse is more successful or more adept than you. Instead of becoming infected with jealousy, focus on the fact that the two of you are a team, and their success is your success. Sometimes, the affected spouse might feel like their relationship has become dull, lopsided, or unfulfilling and seek advice and comfort elsewhere. This is emotional cheating. Find a way to address the issue that has led to impulsive behaviors and fix it.

The non-affected spouse might have reached a point where they begin to resent every moment with the affected spouse. They begin to belittle them or criticize them unfairly, nitpicking every little thing until the affected spouse feels torn to pieces. Contempt for your partner can demoralize them and make them less likely to want to open up to you when things are wrong. Avoid this behavior at all costs. If you feel resentful, try to remind yourself of their good qualities. Do it every day if necessary. The affected spouse might feel tired of being criticized or nagged, and you begin to stonewall yourself to end the seemingly constant criticism. You refuse to engage, and you no longer want to listen to what they have to say, so you put up a cold front. It may be hard to hear their criticism, but the best way to address that is to communicate instead of refusing to engage. You are inadvertently telling your spouse that you don't care what they have to say when you do this.

You might be tempted to shut down and disengage from the world when anxiety runs high. You feel as though it's safer and you can protect yourself by not caring at all. In reality, you're coming across as apathetic to your spouse. They may begin to feel like you don't care, or you're falling out of love, or that they love you more than you love them. Instead of shutting out the entire world, let your spouse in when things are bad. It can be tempting to run away from your problems. You think you'll feel better after running away, but the problems you left behind aren't going anywhere. All you're doing is upsetting your spouse more and avoiding responsibility. It can feel tough to own up to your problems and admit to your mistakes, but it's healthier for your mental well-being and your relationship.

These behaviors can certainly be damaging to the relationship. They can be downright destructive if left unchecked. If your partner does any of these and you feel like they aren't changing, you should seek therapy. Things can change, but only if both partners are willing to put the work in and the effort.

Some of the best ways to manage if one or both of you are affected by anxiety is to seek therapy or counseling to manage your issues. Mental health care has a stigma because many people believe that it's only for "crazy" people or insist that they are too private to talk about things. It might be hard to encourage someone to seek therapy who is resistant. This can stall the progress in a relationship and cause negative feelings and resentment. You need to be sensitive to the other person's mental state and the timing of your discussion. You don't want to start the discussion in front of other people, potentially embarrassing or upsetting them. You also want to be careful not to blurt it out in the middle of an argument or while they've been highly stressed or in a bad mood. They may get defensive and refuse to engage further because they believe they're being labeled. Also, a group-style intervention will simply anger them and make them put up more walls. They may not be comfortable with others knowing or interfering in their problems. Be mindful of choosing a time when they are relaxed, and you're alone. *Tip*: Ask them if they're in a good headspace for you to offer a suggestion. You already know if your loved one is open to the idea of help. You should prepare for a no, or repeatedly hearing no. Start by pointing out their good qualities; you're more likely to appeal to someone who is resistant. You can remind them that they're more than their issues. They don't have to be defined by their mistakes. It gives them a chance to see that working on their issues is just that—working on issues. Make sure they know how important your relationship is with them. They may be more likely to understand that you want to improve the relationship or avoid further damage. Be wary of using ultimatums, though. Get specific about the areas you want to see changes. When people refuse therapy, they may believe they don't have a problem. Avoid being judgmental but let them know the areas that you see could use improvement.

They may be aware they need help but are afraid to seek it because of the stigma around mental health support. Using non-stigmatizing language to support them through their journey can be a way to encourage them.

Here are some examples of phrases and words to use and to avoid when speaking to your partner:

- **Do not use:** *Psycho.* "You're so psycho about this." This can make your loved one feel judged and angry.
- **Do not use:** *Crazy.* "You're acting crazy right now!" Crazy, like psycho, makes people more likely to avoid seeking help if they believe they're being labeled.
- **Do not use**: *Paranoid.* "I can't believe how paranoid you're acting." This may make your loved one feel as though *you* think they're overreacting.
- **Do use:** *I will support you. I'm there for you. You can do this.*
- **Do use:** *You are facing difficulties. You seem to be going through a tough time.*
- **Do use:** *You seem to be mistrustful/fearful right now.*

Sometimes they might not know where to start, or it might feel overwhelming to figure out how to set it up. They might be hesitant about seeing a therapist on their own or exposing their issues in a group session. You can offer to go with them for the first few sessions or sit in the waiting room while they're there. You can ensure them that whatever they talk about in therapy is private, and you won't pry for information. They need to feel that they can work through their issues in a safe, non-confrontational manner. If you're there expecting to hear all about it afterward, they may not want to go for fear of being pushed to talk about something they can barely talk about themselves. Make sure that any information they share with you about their therapy session stays private. Sometimes it's tempting to discuss the issue with a close friend or family member, but if they think you're telling their business, they will be even more reluctant to go.

Going to therapy can be a big deal for many. Ensure you're supportive if they decide they're ready to seek help. Be positive and encouraging, and reinforce their decision with positive affirmations. Reassure them of your love throughout the process. Above all, be patient with them and with yourself. Celebrate your victories together and let go of judgment.

Of course, you and your partner can work on issues together. You can seek therapy to help yourself with areas that need improvement, but what can you do on your own to help minimize your own relationship anxieties? Start with making sure you're practicing self-care. Self-care is a hot buzzword these days, but it just means you need to ensure you put your own oxygen mask on first. Before you can work on relationship issues or help your spouse with their issues, you need to look at yourself and examine how you can help yourself feel safe, happy, and cared for. Next, communicate your needs. It might feel like simplistic advice, but are you truly communicating what you need to your partner? It's possible you're bottling it up or expecting them to be a mind reader. Misunderstandings and anger can be avoided when you are clear with what you need. The uncertainties that cause anxiety can then be eliminated.

One of the biggest sources of anxiety is a fear of the future. You fear not having certainty or stress about things that have yet to happen. Take a step back and try to enjoy the present moment in your relationship. There will always be things to worry about, but you can't spend every second worrying or you'll never enjoy the relationship. Whether you have trauma from a past relationship or worry about being good enough, looking internally at your anxieties can help you discover where they may be coming from. What is causing your stress and worry? How can you manage those anxieties to lessen stress in your current relationship? If you're not doing something to manage the stress and anxieties, you're letting them pile up until you explode on each other. It's important to remember that the two of you are a team and that it's okay to bring your anxieties and stresses to each other to help you cope. You'd be surprised at how your spouse may come up with solutions for problems that you didn't even think of—as part of their ability to think outside the box.

Exercises for couples to manage anxieties

Even if you're not on the brink of divorce, here are a few ways you can come together to connect as a couple that will help your marriage:

- **Exercise One: Write a letter**. Write a romantic letter to your partner that focuses on the positive aspects of your relationship, such as the things that first attracted you or some of your favorite memories. Transition to discussing potential areas for growth near the end. Each of you will then silently read your partner's letter before discussing what you wrote about. This is a helpful way to express to your partner what works and what you like about the relationship while also getting across what you would like to work on.

- **Exercise Two: Emotional check-ins**. Choose three emotions you experienced that day to share. The other partner should reflect on your emotions. Example: "It sounds like you were tired, frustrated, and stressed today." Let your partner share the story behind those emotions. Giving your partner the space to express themselves gives you an idea of how to support your partner in whatever they're going through and give them emotional validation. They will feel supported and heard.

- **Exercise Three: Give daily affirmations**.Take time in the day to share two or three things you appreciate about the other person, even small things. Example: "I appreciate that you made me lunch, and I appreciate that you texted me during your break." Positive affirmations will work as positive reinforcement, and it builds trust and respect between the two of you.

- **Exercise Four: Breathe together.** Sit back-to-back in a comfortable position. Start by focusing on your breathing and notice the movement of your body. Then notice the movement of your spouse's body, focusing on them. Bring your breathing in sync for a few minutes. End with a hug. You're working on being more in sync with this exercise and practicing mindfulness.

- **Exercise Five: Watch romantic shows and movies**. Research shows that couples who watch movies together and discuss them afterward for approximately 45 minutes show improvement akin to couples who go to therapy together. This is because it gives you the practice of communicating about relationship issues in a very low-stakes way. Romantic movies are best as they focus on relationships between couples.

- **Exercise Six: Create a wishlist**. Take turns writing down three or more things you'd like more of or less of in the relationship. Use "I" statements to express your desires and how you would feel if the wishes came true. The wishlist is an exercise that allows the two of you to express your needs while in a calm headspace. You and your partner can also visualize what the relationship could look like if the change occurs.

- **Exercise Seven: "The story I'm telling myself."** This exercise is beneficial when you're in the midst of a conflict and projecting your insecurities onto your partner. For example, instead of being accusatory, i.e. "You spend too much time going out with your friends!" you might say, "The story I'm telling myself is that you'd rather spend time with your friends than with me because I'm annoying you." This can frame your feelings in a way that takes ownership of your feelings and your perception of the situation without casting blame on your partner. This gives your partner the chance to share their side of their story, and you two can work things out together.

Chapter Summary

- Relationship anxieties stem from both partners feeling as if their wants and needs aren't met for whatever reason.

- For the affected partner, it may be due to the symptoms of their disorder that cause them to feel fearful, inadequate or misunderstand things. For the non-affected partner, they may be lonely and stressed from accommodating their partner's needs and feel as if their own aren't met.

- Insecurities, if left unchecked, can lead to downright hurtful behaviors, such as being controlling, contempt, emotional affairs, apathy, and running away.

- Take steps to beat insecurities by finding ways to connect with your partner, such as ensuring you're communicating your needs, watching romantic movies together, practicing mindfulness, and owning up to your insecurities. Therapy is also a great option to work through those issues together or separately.

In the next chapter, we will look at some of the relationship issues that come up, including how to build better social skills and tips for couples to understand each other better, including their nonverbal cues.

Day 3

Improve Relationship Skills

Exercise: Stand or sit comfortably, try to relax, and focus on your breathing. Keep your eyes open. Pick something around you that you enjoy looking at, and keep your gaze focused on that item.

Your thoughts may wander, but let them. The less you worry about your wandering thoughts, the easier it will be for them to leave independently. Keep returning your gaze to the object. Continually try to focus on the object in your vision. You're creating a mindful focus. Try this exercise when you're waiting, such as in traffic or stuck in a long line.

Those with the disorder may struggle with their social skills and managing when it comes to social interaction. They may have underdeveloped interpersonal communication skills and a poor understanding of navigating social situations. As a result,they may come across as abrasive, hurtful, scatterbrained, aggressive, overly emotional, too sensitive, or outright disruptive in social settings. This can interfere not only with the relationship between the two of you but your interpersonal relationships as a couple as well. Their interactions with others may be filled with miscommunications and misunderstandings. It can be stressful when, for example, a parent is uncomfortable letting their child have a playdate with your child because of your spouse. Or, it can be difficult to navigate when your spouse accidentally offends your family at dinner.

ADHD has many effects on the way that people navigate the world and how they understand it. They cannot understand social cues. They may zone out during conversations, and they end up missing important details or agreeing to something that they didn't realize as a result. Forgetfulness can mean that they don't get things done that you expect. Poor organizational skills can make you feel frustrated at the state of how messy the house gets or how disorganized your important paperwork becomes. Their emotional outbursts can hurt your feelings and make you feel like you have to walk on eggshells to avoid their temper. They are also more likely to give in to impulsivity which can mean blurting out inappropriate comments or engaging in reckless or irresponsible behavior.

As the non-affected partner, you have your own difficulties in navigating the relationship between ADHD and your partner. Are you constantly shooting them pointed looks when they speak? Do you criticize them for every small misstep or misspoken word? You could be causing more anxiety in your partner than you realize. Often we observe our spouse's interactions through a filtered lens rather than objectively. Was that joking comment really upsetting, or are you on the lookout for your partner offending people because of past behavior? It's possible you're too ready to jump to everyone else's defense instead of taking a step back and letting your partner navigate the world on their own.

Social skills get developed in childhood and adolescence. Children play pretend to understand the world around them. They copy adults or peers, observe situations, practice, and get feedback to acquire their skills. "They may pick up bits and pieces of what is appropriate but lack an overall view of social expectations. Unfortunately, as adults, they often realize "something" is missing but are never quite sure what that 'something' may be" (CHADD, n.d.). As a result, they may struggle with social acceptance. Peers may have viewed or labeled them as "weird" or pushed them into outcast status growing up. They may have been stuck outside the peer groups which would have led to better development of social skills.

There are many ways in which the disorder can affect a person's ability to navigate social situations and enjoy positive social interactions. The symptoms often hinder one's ability to understand and navigate situations

28

in several key areas. Here are the common challenges most people with ADHD face when it comes to social skills:

- **Challenge #1: Inability to pick up on social cues**. Does it ever feel like everyone around you is in on some kind of joke that you just don't get? Do you feel like you frequently break "unspoken" social rules? It can be challenging to navigate in social situations when your social meter seems broken. For example, you miss out when someone's raised eyebrow indicates that they find your comment in poor taste or accidentally keep interrupting someone trying to tell a story.

  How you can work together: Help your spouse with subtle cues when they're talking over people. Be there to explain jokes they may not understand or reassure them when someone is teasing or being sarcastic.

- **Challenge #2: Trouble keeping friendships.** Some people may experience you as too intense or needy. You are coming across as demanding of their time and attention without realizing it. It can feel like your friendships flame quickly and fizzle out quickly. Do you feel like you have a lot of great connections that don't end up going anywhere? Your symptoms may be causing you to alienate people without realizing it.

  How you can work together: Join a team sport or league together. You'll be there to keep an eye on your spouse while still giving them the space to make their own friendships. This also gets the two of you active and out of the house. Physical activity can be a great way to help manage symptoms of ADHD so it will be easier for your spouse to feel in control in a setting like this because they won't be as stressed about managing their emotions–the exercise will give them the boost they need.

- **Challenge #3: Overreacting.** With ADHD, it can be difficult to control your emotions. There is an impairment in the brain that means the brain itself can't properly regulate your emotional reactions to situations. You end up "overreacting" to something someone has said or done. You have meltdowns when things aren't going well. This can feel offputting to people who don't understand you.

How you can work together: Talk through the things that push your anger buttons the most. Identify how it feels when your anger is reaching critical mass. Then, work on finding ways to mitigate the situation when it's getting to the point of no return.

- **Challenge #4: Being scatterbrained and "unreliable."**
  One of the symptoms of ADHD is the inability to focus on the information being presented. You also have trouble with planning tasks and following through. These can lead to people feeling as though you're unreliable to them and that you can't be counted on when it's important.

  How you can work together: Keep track of the things people have asked of your partner together. Have them write everything down, and the two of you can go over the tasks in the evening to plan out how your spouse will tackle them or how the two of you can work on them together.

Affected adults may struggle with making and keeping friendships and be labeled as "difficult" or "problematic" in work settings or adult peer groups. There is an impairment in the executive functioning of the brain, and, as a result, it may feel impossible to learn the skills that everyone else seems to find innate. It's not an impossible task, however. There are ways to learn to create better social skills that will help both of you. To understand subtext, look for context clues. Observe what people are saying and be aware that their words may have alternative meanings. "We can do it when I'm less busy!" might mean "I'd love to when I have less on my plate." It might also mean "I'm politely brushing you off." Be aware of their body language, tone of voice, or the look in their eyes for clues as to what they might be saying. Spend time observing the choice of words someone uses to understand the meaning behind their words better. If they say, "I would love to go!" that probably means they want to go. "If you want to" might mean it's a reluctant yes or a polite no. Consider the phrase "actions speak louder than words." If they say one thing and do another, it would be smart to consider how their actions reveal their true feelings.

When all else fails, use your spouse as a guide. With your spouse's help, the two of you can work on the way you understand those around you. Ask how their interpretation of a situation compares with your interpretation. This is helpful when you feel like you're constantly getting things wrong. Also, be aware that polite behaviors usually disguise people's real feelings. We have created a society that values being polite over being honest, and oftentimes, people choose to spare your feelings instead of saying how they really feel. To decode them better, observe them. Watch how other people in a social setting are acting or behaving. Look at Pinterest or Google for ideas of how to dress or what to wear in certain social occasions. Be deferent to different cultures and customs. Don't be afraid to ask for help if you're stumped.

When you get really excited, you might be speaking too quickly for others to keep up or get a word edgewise. Slow down and take a deep breath so that people around you can participate in the conversation. You can still share your excitement or passion for a topic but give people room to join in. Another way to help yourself deal with your anxieties in social situations is to add a fidget toy or object that you can play with to help decrease anxiety and excess energy. Sitting still might be hard in a formal setting such as a lecture or theater performance, but a non-distracting fidget toy can give you an outlet. Additionally, before a social event, get out excess energy by doing some light exercise or taking a short walk can burn off excess energy before you leave.

If you feel like you're missing information, look your companions in the eye or set down whatever you're doing to give them your full attention. It might be tempting to send a quick work email while you're on the phone with your friend or text your partner a funny meme while having a long conversation with your mom but these actions can come across as disrespectful because you're ignoring them and missing relevant information. Additionally, consider a social skills coach. There are life coaches and therapists who specialize in helping people build up their social skills. Get in touch with someone you think can help and find a strategy together to work through your most troubling situations.

When it comes to understanding nonverbal communication, people with ADHD definitely have a disadvantage. Still, it's possible the non-affected spouse might also be struggling to understand their partner's nonverbal communication. Both partners give off cues with body language, tone, eye contact, etc. that the other might not be picking up on. This can be damaging to the relationship for both parties. When trying to communicate, you can work on being more open with each other about your feelings, and you can speak to a therapist about what you're struggling to speak about, but it's a whole different story to pick up on the things your partner *isn't* saying.

These are the types of nonverbal communication cues that your partner may be expressing:

- **Facial expression**. Fun fact: The facial expressions for many emotions are the same across almost all cultures. Happiness, anger, sadness, surprise, fear, and disgust are universal. Your face can make many expressions and indicate many kinds of emotions.

- **Body movement and posture**. Your posture can indicate many things, such as pride, annoyance, fatigue, or contempt. People show how they feel in how they walk, stand, sit and hold their heads.

- **Gestures**. People use gestures to communicate many things. You can wave hello or point to show a location. You make an okay sign to indicate agreement or put a palm up to say "stop!" Some gestures that are acceptable in one country might be considered offensive in another. For example, a peace sign facing the wrong way is a rude gesture in the United Kingdom. In some cultures, pointing a single finger is rude; using two fingers is a better way to communicate.

- **Eye contact**. Eye contact is one of the first ways we communicate with others. There's a saying that the eyes are the window to the soul, and your eyes can indicate the way you feel even when the rest of you might be hiding your feelings. Some people find maintaining eye contact important during a conversation as a meter to measure interest and respect.

- **Touch**. We often measure our level of respect or closeness through touch. A firm handshake shows strength. A hug is sometimes uncomfortable if you're not close enough to the person you're touching. We even use touch to indicate our interest in someone. For example, a light touch on the arm can go a long way in flirting with another person.

- **Space**. People can be particular about their personal space. If you've ever been made uncomfortable by someone standing too close or getting into your space during a discussion, you understand how space can be used to communicate.

- **Voice**. More than the words spoken, messages can be communicated through how they are spoken. People can often tell sincerity in your tone of voice or sarcasm or contempt. You can communicate fondness or intimacy depending on how you raise or lower your voice.

The way you communicate using body language or nonverbal cues can affect how other people see and perceive you and how much they like or respect you. Based on nonverbal cues, they may even decide whether or not to trust you. If you've ever heard someone say, "I don't like that person's vibes." Or, "Something about that person makes me distrust them," it's nothing special or magical. It's more than likely due to the unconscious nonverbal signals they give off. When you send negative or confusing signals without intending to, communication can become muddled, and connection and trust become damaged.

Improving your ability to interpret nonverbal communication isn't hard; it's a skill that can be learned like anything else. You and your spouse should start by spending time observing each other throughout the day. How does their posture change when stressed or tired? What is it like when they're happy or excited? Does their tone change when speaking to you about chores?

For the affected spouse, this can be a helpful way to figure out how to understand others' nonverbal cues. For the non-affected spouse, you can start to pick up on nonverbal cues that indicate when your partner is struggling or losing attention or having trouble understanding you. Being more observant can make it easier to figure out how to adapt and change to better meet each other's needs. Don't be shy about expressing your affections. Smile at your spouse, look them in the eye, or reach out and touch them when the mood strikes. Hold their hand when you walk together and give them a hug or kiss when leaving. By showing how you feel without words, you increase your trust in each other.

Make sure you're giving them the attention they deserve. Pay attention to how your partner might feel through their nonverbal cues. Are they crossing their arms? They might be agitated. Are they sighing a lot? They may be sad or depressed. Trying to gain a sense of their feelings this way will help you better understand your partner and improve your communication skills with each other. Additionally, give each other surprise nonverbal affection such as a hug when they are talking to you about their day or hold their hand while you're watching a movie together. Surprises keep the romance alive.

If you observe your partner giving off nonverbal cues that you struggle to interpret, ask if what you're observing is correct. Try to avoid asking, "What's wrong?" and point out your observations. They'll appreciate that you're paying attention to their cues instead of expecting them always to explain themselves. When you're in a disagreement or argument, try to refrain from using negative nonverbal cues like eye-rolling and sighing. Put your phone away when your partner is talking to you. These will eliminate misunderstandings and help avoid escalation of conflict.

To improve your connection with each other, plan a weekly date night or have coffee together every morning. Pick something to do together that encourages you to connect with each other. Be happy to see each other.

When you greet your spouse with warmth and seem genuinely excited to see each other, you're fostering a positive association with coming home.

If you're having problems understanding each other, seek out help from someone who understands relationship issues, like a relationship coach. They can help you learn how to communicate better and understand each other's nonverbal cues and communication. Nonverbal cues can be difficult to master, but with time and practice, you will feel yourself and your spouse learning how to navigate each other's communication much easier. It will even help with people outside of your family, with work, and your friendships. You struggle with maintaining relationships as a couple from the symptoms affecting your spouse. It's easy to blame your partner for "messing up" the relationship, but are you working together effectively to navigate social situations? Are you helping your spouse, or are you waiting until they make a mistake and then berating them about it later? It might feel like waiting to talk to them is the best or the only way to get through to them, but there are actually better techniques the two of you can utilize.

If one or both of you are struggling with your social and interpersonal communication skills, there are ways the two of you can work together to make navigating life as a couple much easier. Helping each other through the difficulties is one of the pillars of a healthy relationship. When you work together, you reinforce that you're a team. Before you go into a social situation, know that one of you might want to leave before the other is ready. Agree on a time that works for the both of you and have a strategy for when it's time to go that saves you both from any stress or embarrassment. Also, make sure you're planning ahead. When you know something is coming up, plan for all eventualities, like forgetting things, running late, ADHD triggers, etc. Having a plan to deal with eventualities will help you both feel more confident.

If you know certain situations highly upset you, try to find a way to avoid them or ways to deal with them. If you're getting tired from socialization, take a break or go somewhere quiet. If you're struggling with ADHD symptoms, step away for a while. If your partner needs to step away for their sanity, don't assume they're abandoning you. If the non-affected partner gently and quietly corrects you, don't assume they're trying to embarrass you. Give each other the benefit of the doubt. Find the quiet areas together that can offer a place for retreat.

Knowing what to say in social situations can be extremely helpful. Prepare scripts ahead of time that you can use to answer common questions that come up or appropriate responses to small talk. Practice small talk with your partner to feel more comfortable. When one of you is having a difficult time or needs space, make sure that the other is covering for you or running interference to help you out. Collaborate as partners to figure out how you can help each other best.

It's also better to navigate social situations by figuring out your priorities. Come together to discuss what your priorities as a couple are. What social situations are necessary, and what is less important? What situations are necessary to navigate as a couple, and what situations can handle just one of you attending?

When things go wrong, develop a code word or gesture that helps out in awkward, uncomfortable, or triggering situations. Use that to quietly indicate when you need help, or you can tell your partner is getting overstimulated. Check in with each other every few hours. If you have an agreed-upon time to leave, check-in within a half-hour and ask your partner if they're still comfortable leaving at the agreed-upon time or if they'd like to stay. Check and make sure they are comfortable and enjoying themselves. Ask and make sure that everything is still going alright. Don't forget also to be aware of any triggers. It can be easy to enter a situation, expecting things to go well, only for an unexpected trigger to pop up. Knowing your partner's triggers ahead of time can help you both navigate when it happens.

It can often feel overwhelming for people with the disorder to navigate new social situations, especially if socialization is important for your partner. Rather than making them go to new events, meet new people, and try new things every week, do one new thing a month or let them spend a limited amount of time socializing while building up their tolerance. Try to push yourself outside your comfort zone from time to time. Even if it feels difficult, sometimes your partner needs to accompany them into a situation you aren't comfortable with. You don't have to do it every day, or even every week, but find activities that are a little out of your comfort zone. Learn about your partner's special interests or as the affected partner, go with them to their college reunion. You two should also ensure that you both have alone time. You both need time to be alone and recharge. Make sure you schedule a time for yourselves each day or each week. Having time to recharge can help when you come back together. You will then feel refreshed and ready to reconnect.

Lastly, there are probably things that you are just more comfortable dealing with than your spouse. For example, one of you might not mind calling the doctor to schedule appointments or taking the food from the delivery driver. One of you might be better at asking for playdates for your children from fellow parents or talking to the school administration. Pick tasks that you can handle and trade for the harder ones for you. These tips will help the two of you navigate the situations that occur when living life as a couple. It's never bad to practice socializing and have contingency plans for when things go awry. Continue working with a therapist for more difficult situations, though.

Consider the following scenarios and how you would use the above tips as a couple to effectively manage what happens:

Scenario #1: Carlos and Andrew are set to attend a weekly family dinner together. Carlos' family is very loving and accepting of their son-in-law, but Andrew, who has ADHD, feels anxious about spending another dinner with Carlos' family. They usually arrive around 5 p.m., but Andrew gets tired of social interaction quickly, and the family typically doesn't start eating dinner until much later in the evening. They are also quick to joke and rib each other. Andrew feels left out because he doesn't always get the jokes. Sometimes, when he jokes back, his jokes don't match Carlos' family's sense of humor and they fall flat or offend the person on the receiving end. Andrew doesn't want to go, but Carlos insists, as it's an important family tradition to have dinner together every Sunday. How would the two of you work together to navigate this dynamic?

Scenario #2: Zahra and Eli are parents to Moses, who is in the third grade. Eli is a social butterfly and often arranges playdates for their son with family friends' children. Eli has been busy lately, and their son has asked mom to arrange a playdate with his best friend Zolan. Mom has ADHD and the thought of calling up Zolan's mom gives her anxiety as she and Abby don't get along. She doesn't know why Abby has a problem with her, but it affects her son's relationship with his best friend. Mom wants dad to do it, but he's about to leave to travel abroad for work and doesn't really have time. Dad wants mom to feel more comfortable arranging playdates and interacting with other parents. How would the two of you handle this?

Scenario #3: Michael and Sophia are newlyweds. Michael has ADHD and has made it clear that he's not very open to new things. He's got a few foods that he likes; he's got a few places in town that he enjoys going to visit, but he mostly stays at home and keeps to himself. Sophia doesn't want to change him, but she does want to try new things here and there. She begs Michael to try a new Indian restaurant that's opened just down the street. Michael reluctantly agrees but ends up not enjoying himself. Sophia is mad that Michael now refuses to try any new restaurants or bars. She ends up going out herself almost every weekend with her friends, while Michael stays at home, lonely without his new wife. How would the two of you handle this situation?

There is no one right answer to each of the scenarios. The answers depend on the shared values and priorities that you have. How you make the situations work is entirely up to you. With each new situation you experience, each unique challenge, you have the opportunity to grow as a couple as you work together to navigate. Some days, it can feel like having ADHD means you don't get to live the lives of a couple that you imagined or that it's ruining your relationships–but you don't have to continue to feel that way anymore.

Chapter Summary

- Symptoms can interfere with your ability to navigate social situations, which can affect your social life. It can feel like your symptoms are getting the better of you, but there are ways to learn to improve and to mitigate when things go wrong.
- Build a social skills toolkit that helps you better understand others and things you can use when you're struggling. Examples include using context clues, looking to your spouse as a guide, and observing their nonverbal cues.
- Nonverbal cues can be particularly difficult for people with ADHD to navigate. Nonverbal cues include eye contact, body language, tone of voice, posture, and facial expressions.
- You can work together on gaining a better understanding of each other's nonverbal cues, which will help the both of you identify and manage when symptoms are becoming an issue.
- Have a plan for potential problems and ways you'll work together to solve them when going into a social situation. Plan an exit strategy, run interference, and find ways to avoid your triggers or get away to a quiet space.

In the next chapter, we'll look at conflicts for affected couples and how to navigate them and resolve them in positive, healthy ways.

Day 4

Resolve Conflicts in a Healthy Way

Exercise: Try this when you're both in the midst of an argument and need a break from the discussion. Take three steps apart from each other, breathe in for four, hold for four, our for six. Repeat three times in a row.

Next, step forward again until you're touching your palms. Let your thoughts go. Focus on the way your partner feels. Imagine what their emotions are at the moment. Try to connect with their body and their emotions. Let yourself focus on them, on their state of being. Do this for five to ten minutes, and then when you're done, resume the discussion.

Understanding how to manage when conflict arises is the cornerstone of any successful marriage. Knowing how to communicate in a healthy manner, how to compromise, how to handle disagreements, and even how to argue successfully are all vital to ensuring a happy life together. With the presence of the disorder though, it can become extremely difficult to manage when conflict arises. The affected partner may have difficulty articulating what is going wrong for them. The non-affected partner might feel as though they struggle to get through when communicating. There are definitely hurdles to get through in an ADHD-affected marriage. The key is to work within the symptoms and not against them.

Conflict exists in every relationship. No relationship is ever going to be one-hundred percent conflict-free. Even the best relationships may struggle with resolving conflict in a healthy manner. We can easily get stuck in a mindset that "I'm right and you're wrong," which doesn't bode well for a productive discussion. It's similar for people with the disorder as well. There is a disconnect for them in which it's difficult to process and understand the emotions and feelings of others. It may seem like they lack empathy, and it's true, to a degree. They also struggle to understand and process their own emotions as well, though. To better manage conflict, it's important to understand how and when conflict normally arises, how to be a good listener, how to argue effectively, and how to be a productive problem-solver.

Conflict arises when you and your partner strongly disagree with one another. The conflict may be unintentional on one partner's end, or one or both of you are unaware of the conflict. When situations arise that have us feeling a lot of emotion, we may be provoked or upset by others' reactions. However, no discussion is going to be productive if you cannot understand what your emotions are saying. You're putting the onus on your partner to fix things, and that's unfair to them. You could be unintentionally expecting your partner to be a mind reader because you can't understand what you're feeling but expect them to be able to resolve the conflict themselves.

Conflict can arise when one partner feels the other isn't being honest, when you disagree about values, or when you have strongly differing opinions. The things you two disagree on can range from values and beliefs such as whether or not to have children, how to raise them, how to manage finances, where you want to live, etc., to smaller decisions such as what to have for dinner, where to go on vacation, to trivial things like who fed the dog last or whose turn it is to empty the dishwasher. Conflict can be normal and good—such as when you're standing up for yourself in defense of your beliefs or against injustice—but it can also be problematic when conflict arises too often. Again, it's about learning to strike a balance for both of you.

When conflict arises, the first difficulty is often understanding where it's coming from. Discovering what causes conflict among you will help you understand yourself and each other better. For people with the disorder, their emotions can often become more intense and exaggerated. This is because there is an issue with the brain that prevents you from regulating intense emotions the same way that neurotypical people can. You literally cannot control how intense the emotions feel. You're also extremely sensitive to criticism and disapproval. This is often called Rejection Sensitive Dysphoria (RSD), which can cause symptoms similar to anxiety and depression when faced with feeling rejected or criticized. What you can control, though, is how you work through those intense emotions at the moment. Sometimes you need to take a step back before you blow up at your partner or lash out to hurt them.

One way to do that is to keep a journal where you write down your feelings. By journaling, you can begin to understand yourself better. For example, you'll be able to understand why you were so upset when you heard slight uncertainty in your spouse's tone when you suggested pizza for dinner or why you were so upset when they criticized how you loaded the dishwasher. You might also want to take space during the heat of the moment. You'll avoid lashing out in anger and defensiveness if you walk away. You may feel like your anger is making you want to explode and walking away can allow you to calm down and reassess the situation. You'll be able to come back to the discussion with a greater understanding and be able to work through things more calmly and rationally. It can definitely sting when our partner isn't excited about something we suggest, or we feel like they're being overly critical of the way we do things around the house.

As the non-affected spouse, you could also be unintentionally pushing their symptom triggers by the way you approach your critiques. If you're trying to comment on something, it might sound more like criticism, bringing up feelings of shame and defeat. If you're constantly questioning them because you don't trust their memory, you are probably pushing them to feel demoralized when they forget something. When you criticize them about their spending habits, they will feel as though they can't be trusted with a single cent without being questioned. It's frustrating when your partner struggles with things that come easier to you, and it's easy to dismiss their symptoms as a failure on their part to step up. You ought to examine the way you approach them, though. Triggering their symptoms of shame, guilt, and anxiety will not correct the problem and will only damage the relationship over time.

If you come home and notice the dishes aren't done, despite asking, you use facts to guilt them, "The dishes aren't done." They are aware that they didn't complete the task asked. Or, if they genuinely forgot, they feel plenty of guilt without needing more, "I asked you to get the dishes done and you didn't listen." You nag them, repeatedly asking, "When are you going to do the dishes?" throughout the evening.

Instead of nagging, guilting, or shaming them, ask them "What would it take to get the dishes done?" People with the disorder often struggle with executive dysfunction, so a simple task like the dishes can feel inordinately overwhelming. For a neurotypical person, a task like doing the dishes might involve simply getting up and washing the dishes. For someone with ADHD, however, doing the dishes can be many steps, such as gathering the dishes around the house, ensuring there's enough soap, finding the sponges, putting away dishes from the dishwasher or drainer, soaking the plates with food residue, organizing the dishes into piles, etc. One task, in their minds, can feel like ten or more tasks. This doesn't even account for the fact that a task such as dishes involves standing still for a long time, which is one of the more difficult aspects of the disorder.

Recognizing the difficulty of approaching tasks is a helpful way to minimize conflict in the relationship. Once you're aware of how to work within the disorder's symptoms instead of against them, you'll discover that your spouse is more than capable of accomplishing anything you ask. One tip for dealing with an affected partner is to give them a to-do list. This is helpful as it gives them a visual reminder of the tasks required. It also eliminates the possibility of forgetting how verbal requests are often forgotten. Additionally, people with the disorder tend to enjoy checking off items on a to-do list. It gives them a boost of serotonin to visually see things getting done. Another tip is to help them out by sitting with them while they work. Body-doubling, as it's called, is a great way to help keep them focused. You can also help by working with them to help them break the task down into the steps needed so it feels less overwhelming.

It's also prudent to pick your battles. For example, if your partner cannot ever seem to remember to put their clothes in the hamper, but they're great at many other things, it might be time to let that battle go. It's not worth spending years of your life unhappy over something very minor.

When you let go of the small things, your partner will also understand how important the big issues are to you. You'll also spend less time stressing yourself out. You'll gain more respect for your spouse as well. When you stop thinking of them as the enemy or focusing on all their little mistakes, you'll find yourself able to open your heart and fall in love with them all over again.

For times when it's harder to love your spouse or when you feel like their disorder is getting hard to separate from who they are as a person, you need to find a way to step back and reconnect. Start pointing out to yourself the things you like about them. Focus on the things you fell in love with. There will be days when you're stressed out because you're trying to juggle many plates in the air, and it feels like your spouse has let you down one time too many, but that's when it's most important to remind yourself of the good. Resentment builds where there is no love. If you're serious about making things work, you need to foster that love inside of you.

Another often unexplored cause of conflict between couples is the fact that people with the disorder often–consciously or unconsciously–create conflict as a way to get a boost of serotonin and dopamine. Their brains crave it and this stimulates the brain in ways that other things just can't. They may deny it, but it's not unheard of for a partner to look for ways to stir trouble. Again, this may not be a conscious thing on their part. "When the ADHD brain doesn't have enough stimulation, it looks for ways to increase its activity. Being angry or negative has an immediate stimulating effect on the brain." (Amen, 2020) There are a few ways that people with the disorder will engage their partner in drama games. One way they do this is by picking on others to get a rise out of them or upset them. Does your significant other pick something that upsets you to constantly tease you about, even after you've asked them to stop numerous times? Do you end up snapping or getting angry with them over that? You're giving their nervous system a shot of adrenaline, which raises your partner's heart rate and brain activity.

Another method they use is pushing your buttons to the point where you start yelling or screaming at them. People with the disorder can pick up your most vulnerable spots and target them. Being less reactive to this can

44

even increase the behavior at first. They want to push and push until you explode. Some people with the disorder end up being more argumentative and oppositional. They get a rush from saying "no" to your request or ignoring it completely. They can't step up until you're arguing with them or fighting over it. It's not that they're always actively trying to hurt you or the relationship; it's that their brains don't want them to stop. They have to learn how to control this urge and curb it when it's popping up in full force. They have to learn how to work around the urge to defy or ignore you. They need to get trained out of that behavior, working with a therapist or counselor, or through consequences that take away the desire to engage in the negative behavior. The affected partner isn't necessarily behaving badly on purpose, but they are engaging in behaviors that can destroy the foundation of the marriage.

After identifying the source of the conflict, you can now begin to understand how to eliminate them. One of the biggest sources of conflict in a marriage, especially one affected by ADHD, is that one or both partners feel as though they aren't being heard. For example, one spouse might feel as though they've done everything in their power to explain why they're upset, but unless they know they're being heard, they have no confidence the issue will be resolved satisfactorily. As an example, if Bob is upset that Sara repeatedly ignores him when he asks her to text him after she leaves the office, and Sara says she's listened but continues to forget to do so, Bob is going to feel as though his words went in one ear and out the other.

Becoming a better, more active listener is the next step for both of you. Most of us want to be heard, but we may not listen when someone else speaks. Are you an active listener? Active listening is more difficult for people with the disorder, but it's a skill that can be learned like anything else. Active listening means stopping anything else you're doing when someone wants to talk to you. It means putting down the phone, waiting to send a text, or pausing your video game. It means giving your partner eye contact or demonstrating body language that shows you're engaged in the conversation.

While it might feel tough to engage in a lengthy conversation, there are a few ways you can help yourself remain active. Use a fidget toy that helps you stay focused but doesn't distract your partner. Agree to a time limit for the conversation. Discuss the issue for no more than twenty minutes and then agree to pick it up again later if it's still unresolved. By giving yourself a time limit you're both more likely to focus on what's important. You can also work with your ADHD by going into a quiet, non-stimulating environment to have a discussion. Trying to engage someone with the disorder in a serious talk while there's a lot of environmental stimulation in the background will just be counterproductive. You're more likely to feel frustrated than engaged.

Active listening also ensures you foster a sense of safety and trust in each other. This means that you know you won't be treated badly, punished, or humiliated for speaking up. The two of you are comfortable laying it all on the line and working through problems together without fear of repercussions or backlash. If you want to show you're actively listening and that their concerns are treated seriously, make sure you ask good questions. Asking clarifying questions also helps you stay engaged. With a disorder like ADHD, you may struggle to retain the information, so don't be afraid to repeat the information back to your partner. This allows them to correct or verify what you have heard. Being engaged will help you minimize how your disorder interferes when your partner is attempting to communicate with you.

Another reason conflict can arise in your marriage is because your spouse wants you to put more effort in to be an equal partner or often feels like they're in a parent-child relationship with you. They want you to take a more active role in solving the problems that arise, but you inadvertently push the narrative that you don't care because you're not stepping up. Are you taking the initiative to help when without being asked? Are you finding ways to figure problems out on your own, or waiting for your partner to fix things? Are you engaging in active problem solving, or passively waiting for the issue to just go away on its own? Being an adult can feel tough some days. You have responsibilities that you never imagined, and sometimes you just want to get away from it all. The problem comes when you run away from your responsibilities in a relationship. You're now leaving all the problems at your partner's feet, and it's wildly unfair. Feeling overwhelmed doesn't give you a pass to do nothing.

Starting today, you're going to learn how to become a problem solver and you're going to engage in active problem-solving. When you're unsure how to do something, look it up instead of asking your spouse. There are thousands upon thousands of YouTube videos, WikiHow articles, and blog posts that detail exactly how to do a vast number of adult tasks. No one is born knowing how to do everything, they have to learn, and you are more than capable of doing so. When you feel like your spouse is nagging you, find out what the real issue might be. There's always an underlying issue behind a seemingly petty one. For example, if your spouse is constantly nagging you about taking out the trash, there could be an underlying concern for bugs or rodents, they could be worried about how sanitary things are with children around, or they could be stressed about something outside of their control and having the trash taken out every night is something they feel they can control.

Whatever is the underlying issue, help them by making sure they feel secure in coming to you with their problem. The disorder often means that your partner doesn't always feel comfortable coming to you for help. The ironic thing is that people with the disorder are often great problem solvers. They can think outside the box, look at problems from a different perspective and see things others don't. It's important to hone that problem-solving skill for your relationship. It's useful when coming up with ways to tackle problems in the office, but it's just as helpful in tackling issues at home.

Start by being a safe place for your partner to come to with their issues. Being dismissive or critical won't help. Instead, give them space to be heard. Avoid the urge to be defensive or to dismiss their concerns out of hand. You can't resolve conflict if one or both of you are resistant to hearing what is being communicated. Being a good problem-solver means being a good listener. If they come to you with something they see as an issue, be willing to hear them out before speaking. Sometimes we're ready to jump in and explain things or defend ourselves before we've even let our partner finish talking. Instead, ask if they've said everything they wanted before you jump in. It's not only respectful, but it shows that you're listening instead of just waiting to jump in.

When you're given the opportunity to speak, now it's time to show you can be a problem-solver. Start by setting aside your feelings and your ego. It doesn't mean ignoring your feelings or putting yourself second to your partner. It means leaving your emotions out of the equation and treating it like a problem to be solved analytically. When you approach the problem critically, you're less likely to feel anxious or upset about the situation. You're an engineer here to fix something that's not working. First, identify whatever the problem is that's giving you both trouble. Then, try to figure out what's causing the issue. Often it's not just a matter of the affected spouse being the instigator but a breakdown in communication or expectations.

Think up several possible ways to solve the problem. Look over the options and think about what might work. If A doesn't work, have B, C, and D as backup plans. Choose the solution you feel will work best for the problem. Think through the possible outcomes for each before choosing the right one. Then, put that chosen plan into place and watch to see if that works. If not, go back to the drawing board. Continually check to make sure that the solution still works over time. If not, try another avenue. If you're still struggling, seek outside help like advice from a friend or family member.

Here is an example of the way that one couple worked on their conflict resolution together:

Hannah and Jamie have been married for just over a year. Jamie has ADHD and was diagnosed young. She started medication for it in elementary school and took it regularly throughout school until college. After that, she decided to go off it for a break, and that's when she met Hannah. Jamie is currently unmedicated but does her best to manage her symptoms with exercise and meditation. Hannah has noticed that lately Jamie has been busy with school and work and hasn't been exercising as much as she used to. She's also been so tired that she goes to bed early every night, skipping her nightly meditation. Jamie has also been more snappy with her wife. Hannah has tried to make things easier for her wife while she's in school by taking over most of the household duties, only asking her to contribute to a few tasks. Lately, though, Jamie hasn't even been doing those. Instead, she's been coming home and watching

YouTube videos after work and procrastinating on homework until the last minute.

Hannah has tried not to complain because she understands that her wife is busy, but she gets to a point where she starts to resent being in charge of the entire household and working 40-plus hours a week. It feels like her wife can't be bothered to help. She doesn't know what to do anymore. Things reach a boiling point when Hannah asks Jamie to pop a frozen pizza in the oven after a long day of work. She comes home, ready to eat, only to find out that not only did Jamie ignore her text, but the kitchen was a huge mess, so even if she wanted to put a pizza in the oven, it would take time to clear away the mess enough to do so. They end up in a fight, yelling at each other, and Jamie leaves the house in a huff.

Hannah and Jamie are in a conflict. Hannah is fed up with her wife and feels as though she's bent over backward to accommodate Jamie's schedule with no consideration in return. She also feels like her wife has been more argumentative and irate lately, making her difficult to live with. When Jamie cools off, they come back and sit down together to talk about things. She lays it out for Jamie, explaining how she feels. Jamie takes the opportunity to listen to what her wife has to say, giving her space to talk about her feelings and vent her frustrations without interrupting. When Hannah is done speaking, Jamie explains that because of her workload, she's been too exhausted to take time for herself and has been taking out her emotions on her wife. She owns up to the problem, understanding that she's been difficult to live with lately.

Hannah also acknowledges that she could have been better at communicating her needs in a way that works with her wife's ADHD. She understands that nagging Jamie and getting angry hasn't solved the problem for either of them. Jamie admits that she wants to fix things, and she realizes that while she used to have time to exercise a lot and meditate, she no longer has that same time, and her ADHD has been getting worse. She pinpoints the problem at the source. The next step she takes is brainstorming with her wife to develop solutions for her problem. She suggests they take walks on the weekends together, thereby spending time together and giving Jamie some exercise. Hannah likes that but points out that Jamie needs more than a few weekend walks. Jamie thinks it over and decides that the best solution to the problem at the moment is for her to go back on medication. She knows that without the time to exercise and meditate, she can't function as well, and since she has so much on her plate, she decides that she'll talk to her doctor.

The two of them looked at the problem objectively. Hannah didn't blame Jamie for the state of their relationship, and Jamie took responsibility for her part in the problem. They were able to get to the heart of the issue together. They could have worked on fixing those small issues together, hoping that things would change, but they realized that there was a bigger issue at play--namely that Jamie was feeling like her entire life was getting out of control. Jamie knew that if she wanted to fix things, it wouldn't be one simple fix either. Medication would help, but they would still need to work through the issues that were cropping up.

They tried medication, and it definitely started making a difference. The issues didn't completely disappear but things were more manageable for Jamie on the day-to-day. They scheduled a check-in within a month of starting medication so that they could honestly talk about how things were going. Hannah was pleased with the improvement but noted that Jamie was still constantly tired at the end of the day. Jamie admitted that working and going to school was tough for her, even with medication. They mutually decided for Jamie to quit her job. Hannah made enough to support them both, and Jamie knew she would make more once she graduated, and her focus on school, for now, was the best for their relationship and Jamie's mental health.

They knew that the issue was bigger than both of them and that it wasn't about who was right or wrong—it was about coming together to look at the problem, pinpoint where the issue was exactly, and brainstorm ways to fix it. Often in high-conflict situations, things aren't as black and white as "My spouse is ignoring me and only focusing on themselves!" Or "My partner won't ever listen to me!" Getting to the heart of the matter is vital. It means that you can eliminate the growth at the root, instead of getting bogged down by smaller, petty issues. If the problem can be eliminated at the source, many of the smaller issues will also be eliminated as well.

Chapter Summary

- Conflict arises when two or more people have different opinions and can't come together on them without work. For example, an affected marriage can have conflict because of the way the symptoms present–difficulty with understanding other's points of view, difficulty with following through, lack of empathy for the other's emotions, and troubles with self-esteem affecting criticism.

- The best way to handle conflict is to become a better listener and a better problem solver. Becoming a better listener requires setting aside your ego and engaging in active listening. Active listening means staying engaged, asking good questions, and using affirmative language to show you sympathize.

- Becoming a better problem solver includes admitting to the problem, looking at the options, figuring out the best ones, trying that out through trial and error, and continually checking in to ensure that the solution still works.

Do you feel like the problem with your conflicts lies with how you communicate? If it's a communication issue causing conflict, the next chapter will discuss communication. You'll learn how to communicate with each other.

Day 5

Improve Communication

Exercise: Do this at the end of each week. Sit in a comfortable position, in an intimate place for the two of you. Bedroom, couch, anywhere you feel comfortable. Face each other. You can hold hands if you wish. Look each other in the eye, breathing in and out deeply until you both feel calmness and stillness inside.

Each of you takes turns listing out the things you were grateful the other did that week. Start with broad things such as "I'm grateful you were by my side every night at bedtime" and work down to more specific examples such as "I'm grateful you made a delicious dinner on Friday." Do this 5 to 10 times. Repeat the exercise each week to build gratitude into your daily life.

Do you feel like you have to repeat yourself for your spouse to understand or comprehend what you're saying? Do you feel your partner often gives you only vague information about their day? Maybe you experience issues with your spouse explaining themselves clearly—especially when they've done something to upset you.

One of the ways that ADHD affects relationships is in the area of communication. Marriages affected by ADHD can have higher instances of miscommunication, especially misunderstandings, hurt feelings, and lack of communication. More than that, there are also ways in which we could be misunderstanding our partner's intentions or even misinterpreting them. It can feel like the disorder hijacks your conversations, leading you to interrupt people, or your lack of attention span causes you to miss important details in conversations. It's possible to hog the conversation, especially if you feel passionate about the topic, leading others to feel like they have no space to talk.

Whatever it is, you may feel like trying to fix it has your brain working against itself. That's true—and it's because of your executive dysfunction. Executive functions are part of the cognitive processes of your brain—kind of like your brain's manager—that regulate and control certain abilities such as self-control, organization, time management, memory, and emotional regulation. Executive dysfunction is "a term used to describe the range of cognitive, behavioral, and emotional difficults which occur as a result of [a] disorder or a traumatic brain injury." (Rodden & Saline 2022) People who struggle with executive dysfunction struggle with things like staying on task, planning, staying organized, and the ability to regulate their emotions. They also struggle with self-restraint and self-awareness. These are all difficulties that can add up to much bigger problems in relationships.

As marriage is a give-and-take endeavor, it can feel as though the non-affected partner is doing all the giving while the disordered partner is doing all the taking. When the affected partner is upset, they may lash out instead of calmly expressing themselves. It is a real struggle for the affected partner to regulate their emotions at the moment, and this definitely can lead to hurt feelings. Additionally, the affected partner could be struggling to articulate whatever is affecting or bothering them that contributes to the issues they're experiencing. They also struggle with non-verbal communication, as we discussed on day three. As a result, they don't understand how or why they have upset you or how you're expressing your frustration.

People with the disorder also struggle to process information and tend to internalize issues. They often struggle with comorbidities such as anxiety and depression. They take what you're saying as an attack on them or disappointment in who they are as a person. Their brains want to assign meaning to everything to understand and look for ways to pick apart whatever you communicate. Anxiety and depression also look for ways to turn their thoughts against themselves. It's a cycle perpetuated by past negative experiences.

It's not that they're looking for ways to be hurt; it's that their brains struggle to process. For some, it's about understanding when they're talking too much and not listening enough. For others, it's about finding the words to communicate how they feel. It will take baby steps to improve communication, but it can be done. The best way to go about it is to understand that communication is a two-way street. It's not going to be easy to communicate if the affected partner feels bad about how they communicate. And it's not going to be easy to manage if the affected partner doesn't communicate at all.

As a child, did you ever get a report card that said, "Good student, but they talk too much in class"? Were you labeled a chatterbox growing up? Do you accidentally dominate conversations? Talking too much or in excess is one of the disorder's symptoms. You may not even realize you're doing it. It can be easy for you to go on and on if you're excited about the topic. Talking too much could be driving your spouse up the wall, though. They feel as if they can't get a word in edgewise, or they feel like you're not taking time to listen to them. Do you rush to explain yourself and end up overexplaining? You're probably so eager to fix the situation that you're not letting your partner communicate their needs.

It's okay to be excited or passionate about something. It's okay to want to explain yourself when situations crop up. It's also necessary to let the conversation flow a little more. One way to combat it when you feel like you're talking too much is to ask questions after you've spoken for a few sentences. This lets the other person have a say and gives the conversation a more natural flow. If you repeat the things they say to yourself silently, you can keep focused on listening to your partner instead of talking. When dealing with a discussion or argument, if you feel like you're talking too much, it's okay to pause and ask your partner if they have something to add. This ensures that you both get a fair chance to speak.

Sometimes you do your best not to talk too much, but you end up interrupting anyway. When you interrupt others, it can come across as rude, thoughtless, or bossy. You make others feel like you don't give them enough respect to listen. It can be hard; you get so excited that you want to jump in, or you worry that they'll move the conversation along before you get a chance to add your piece. You also worry that you'll forget what you have to say if you don't say it right then and there. Try to become more aware of how often you're interrupting others when they're speaking. Count the times you interrupt without meaning and work on not interrupting more than a certain amount of times. If you do catch yourself interrupting, take ownership. A simple "I'm sorry for interrupting, what were you going to say?" goes a long way. During conversations, take a deep breath, slowly, and then exhale if you find yourself overwhelmed. You can calm yourself down so the urge to interrupt lessens. With your spouse, give each person a chance to talk without interruption. Cover your mouth with your hands if you need to, or sit on your hands as a reminder not to speak until it's your turn. This works most effectively during a serious discussion, but it can be a good way to practice for less important topics as well.

One reason you are often interrupting is that people with the disorder tend to struggle with short-term memory, and they know if they don't speak as quickly as possible when they have a thought, it will likely be gone before they get a chance to express it. It can certainly be good to quickly express an important thought, but interrupting to do so is considered rude. If you're prone to forgetting, write things down ahead of time, jot a note for yourself on your phone or ask politely to interrupt. Saying "I'm sorry to interrupt, I have a question/I have a thought" can help the other person feel that you're not trying to hog the conversation but understand that you have something to contribute.

If you wait until it's your turn, you also give yourself time to think over what you want to say and decide whether or not it's important to the conversation. Blurting things out that are hurtful, inappropriate, or unhelpful is common with the disorder, and sometimes it's best to take a step back and ruminate over what you want to say.

There's an acronym that can be helpful here. T.H.I.N.K. Ask yourself:

- (T) Is it True?
- (H) Is it Helpful?
- (I) Is it Inspiring?
- (N) Is it Necessary?
- (K) Is it Kind?

Using T.H.I.N.K before you speak can eliminate a lot of hurt feelings, insecurities, and verbal missteps. Try to use the acronym when you're going into a difficult conversation with your spouse. We all get into bad habits of using words that hurt. ADHD amplifies that because you lack the ability to filter unless you work at it. The disorder can make you feel as though you want to lash out, and one of the ways we lash out as humans is to throw exaggerated claims using "always" and "never" which can derail the conversation and put our partner on the defensive. It's very rarely true that someone always or never does something, so try to eliminate that from your vocabulary when you're having a discussion.

On the other hand, you could be struggling to come up with the words to say to express yourself when you're communicating. You feel as though you want your partner to understand you, but the words won't come out, or you use the wrong words, which leads to misunderstandings. When that happens, take a deep breath and work on organizing your thoughts. Ask for a pause so you can collect yourself. If the words still aren't coming to you, ask to talk later. Write down what you want to say and when you reconvene, have your partner read them to you so they can understand what you've said. Ask what they are getting from your words. This will stop any miscommunication in its tracks by cutting it off at the source.

You don't have to resolve every problem straight away. Get in the habit of calling for a time-out when you feel flustered, angry, upset, embarrassed, or anxious and you can't communicate what you want to say right away. By giving yourself time, you are not only letting yourself collect your thoughts, but you give yourself time to calm down as well and deal with the initial feelings that are bombarding you. This is especially relevant during long conversations. ADHD makes it difficult to process and communicate during long discussions. When you find yourself stuck in a long conversation, try to ask for a break or set yourself up for success ahead of time. Eliminate distractions before you talk. Turn off the television, put down the phone, and close the door to avoid interruptions. Ask if you can record the conversation to listen to it again later. This is especially good practice if you're forgetful and you want to remember the important things your partner brought up or important details that you're likely to forget.

Long conversations can be difficult. With ADHD, you zone out, even if you know you want to listen. You know that you're likely to miss important information when you zone out. It's tempting to let yourself zone out. It can even be helpful, to a degree. You're more likely to pay attention if your brain can take "breaks," so to speak. Unfortunately, you end up missing important information or details. Trying to sit through a long conversation without breaks is possible with some of the tools and tips mentioned in the chapter *Day One*, but at some point, you have also to decide if it's worth putting both of yourselves through that stress. Ultimately, working with the disorder is better than working against it. Breaking important conversations up into smaller, more manageable chunks is a lot easier on both partners and a much healthier way of dealing with issues than trying to work through a list of problems over the course of several hours.

Do you, as the non-affected spouse, feel as though you're constantly communicating only to realize that what you said went in one ear and out the other? Do you get angry or anxious that your spouse won't remember what you tell them and nag them so they will remember? Are you using their ADHD against them or working with them? It's easy to blame your spouse for not doing their part, but it's on both of you to communicate better. If you were sick with an illness that meant you were limited in what you could do around the house, would you be upset if your spouse put unfair expectations on you and then got fed up when you couldn't meet those expectations? The disorder is also an illness–it's a mental illness. It means that there are limitations to what your partner can do, and you are putting them to the same unfair standards. In this case, there are no physical limitations, but there are things that you need to work around.

If you desire to have them remember certain important dates, and you know that remembering things is a challenge, help them remember. Set up a household calendar, text them reminders, work with them, and don't expect that they always get it right on their own. If they often interrupt you during conversations, instead of yelling at them or scolding them like a child, gently put your hand on theirs and remind them that it's still your turn. Treat them like an adult but give them the grace that their disorder sometimes needs. Then, when you feel like nagging or berating, take a step back and ask yourself the T.H.I.N.K. questions—is it true, helpful, inspiring, necessary, or kind? Treating each other with more respect will go a long way toward rebuilding the bridge between the two of you, and it can head issues off at the pass.

When you find your spouse struggling to find the right words to say, give them the space they need to speak without interrupting or trying to guess what they might be saying. If their words come out wrong, realize that they don't intend to hurt you, they are struggling to explain the complex way their brain communicates thoughts and emotions to them. Imagine a train going from Los Angeles, CA to Charlotte, NC. On a map, they appear to be almost a straight line across. A journey like that, by train, wouldn't take very long at all in a straight line. However, trains make frequent stops. A journey that looks like two days on a train might be more like ten days with all the stops. The ADHD brain is similar. Thoughts move slower and less linearly for those with the disorder. It takes longer to work from one thought to the next. Being patient with them as they work through their train of thought, no pun intended, will allow them to think through what they want to say. Additionally, ADHD brains are adept at looking at a problem and working through solutions. Giving them time to think will let their brain pick up ideas along the way and arrive at their destination with a fresh solution that neither of you has thought of yet.

The two of you can also work together to find better ways to communicate—ways that work for your unique situation. For example, if you realize that you struggle with verbal communication, you might write each other letters that lay out the words that you can't get out. It gives you both a chance to explain your side without interruption. You should communicate this way only after giving yourself time to calm down. Communication should never be done via text message or email when you're angry, as there is no tone indicator via written communication. If you need to communicate more urgently but still struggle, sit next to each other while you text. This way you have the opportunity to collect your thoughts but can also clarify face to face as well. Another communication hack for affected couples is creating rules for engagement. When you create rules for your discussions or discourse, you are less likely to end up in yelling matches. As an example, create a rule that no name-calling is allowed. If name-calling comes up, agree that the other party calls a time-out immediately, and both parties must walk away.

You could also have a rule that states no use of extreme statements like "always" and "never." If those happen, call for a pause. These statements are often masks for underlying issues, and you want to get to the heart of the issue. It may seem like the frustration is in the instance of the "always" and "never," but there's something deeper going on. When one person uses those extremes, they feel as though their concerns aren't heard. They feel you aren't taking their concerns seriously and don't feel respected. You can also encourage each other to share what you *need* instead of what you *expect*. Emphasizing the facts of what you need instead of putting demands or expectations on them will turn them from feeling defensive into feeling proactive.

Reboot. Sometimes a discussion turns into an argument or a screaming match, and it feels like everything goes wrong in those instances. When the two of you are calming down, give yourselves time to reflect on what went wrong. Often, dealing with the disorder means that you get good at self-reflection in hindsight. You often think of the witty remarks you might have made or better strategies you could have used to diffuse the situation. You also reflect on the mistakes you made that you would do differently if given a chance. Use that to your advantage here. Come back together, and each of you should discuss how *you* would have handled things differently to ensure a positive experience. Extend an olive branch, swallow your pride and admit when you're wrong. There's always opportunities to grow and do better in the future.

Even when we try our best, things still seem to be getting out of control. You can communicate all day long, but nothing will change if the other person won't listen or can't hear what you're saying. Do you feel like you've had all the talks, heard all the promises and nothing is changing?

Then, it might be time to seek out professional help. A marriage and family therapist or counselor is trained in handling communication issues and conflict resolution between couples. Seeking out therapy is a good option when the two of you are having more fights than discussions and more arguments than resolutions.

Seeking out help can sometimes feel like admitting defeat. That's not the case, though. We are only human, and in the end, we are limited in our abilities to change without outside help. You get stuck in the mindset that airing your problems is wrong or will somehow magnify them if you admit what's happening. You think that allowing a stranger to know intimate details of your relationship is wrong. You feel like there's no helping the two of you, and going to a therapist won't fix what's broken. These mindsets will hold you back from working through the communication issues preventing you from having a happy, successful relationship. Bringing up the issues in couples counseling can certainly be difficult. But marriage does take work, and good relationships are ones where both partners are ready to do the work.

If you find yourself at a crossroads, especially if you're contemplating divorce, you feel as though there are only two options in front of you. Do you stay, knowing you're unhappy, or do you leave to find happiness elsewhere? You feel stuck and afraid of making the wrong choice. You know it's time to seek help when the issues are bad enough that you're contemplating leaving, but here are some of the other signs it's time to seek help:

- Conflicts have begun to escalate and nasty words are hurled around.
- There is a bridge of emotional distance between you that you can't cross.
- You feel as though you are losing trust in your partner.
- Your partner's own self-worth and fears of abandonment are interfering with your ability to properly communicate without escalation and accusations.
- Your difficulties with in-laws, work stress, or friends are bleeding into your ability to be open and honest with each other.

- You two can't come together to agree on fundamental issues such as parenting styles.
- You feel unsupported or have difficulty opening up to each other emotionally.
- You worry that your partner's addictions (alcohol, drugs, porn, or shopping habits) are getting out of control.
- One or both of you experienced a difficult or traumatic upbringing that has emotionally wounded you and made conflict a bigger deal when it arises.
- Undiagnosed depression or anxiety is making it hard for one partner to function.
- Your ADHD is becoming unmanageable to the detriment of your life and relationship.

If one or more of these issues are causing a rift and making you unhappy enough to consider leaving, a good therapist can work with you to help you through these and potentially save your relationship. You will be able to shine a light on the underlying issues and access feelings that were buried or ignored. Even if your marriage isn't on the rocks, counseling can be a huge positive for the relationship. An ounce of prevention is better than a pound of cure, as the saying goes. You want to stop problems in their tracks before they become bigger and more unmanageable–before they can start to crack the foundation of your relationship. You'll learn how to develop healthy relationship skills, solve communication issues, and learn how to communicate better. Like getting your oil changed every 3,000 miles, going to a "couples check-up" in therapy is good for the health of the relationship. You can get an assessment of how your relationship is doing and work through any minor issues or solve small communication problems with help.

The two of you also get the opportunity to set goals for the relationship. You can set a goal that you work towards, and once you feel confident that goal is met, you can discontinue therapy or just go for regular check-ins every so often. Therapy provides a safe space for the two of you to discuss things that you are having difficulty addressing on your own–everything from communication disconnect to differing on values and even intimacy issues. For example, if you're having communication issues, you may still be stumbling because there's a difference between communication and effective communication. This is especially relevant when major life changes are on the horizon, such as deciding to go back to school, having a baby, taking a new job opportunity, or moving house. These types of transitions can destabilize couples due to the stress and pressure that comes from making decisions and planning things out.

Therapy can offer a great deal of help in many areas but finding the right therapist is essential. You need to do your research together before finding a therapist. Look up the things that they focus on and determine if those align with you as a couple. Some counselors offer religious-based help and some offer help for couples in all areas, including sex therapy. Finding the right therapist is a bit like dating, though. You won't know they're right for you until you sit down with them and meet them. It's okay to decide after the first visit, or the first couple of visits, that the therapist isn't a good fit. You may need to try a few out before finding one you connect with. Pay attention to their approach to your issues. You want to ensure their communication style and the rationale behind their questions makes sense to you. If you're not comfortable opening up to them, you won't do the work they ask. Any homework they assign should explained and make sense.

Once you've found a therapist that you both like, encourage each other to continue seeing the therapist both alone and together until you feel you're reaching your communication goals and you both feel as though you've made sufficient progress on your issues. Continuing individual therapy might also be helpful, even beyond reaching your couple's goals. You get the chance to work through issues that compromise your communication with someone qualified to help. Leaning on your spouse for support is always helpful, but some issues are bigger than they can deal with.

Communication can be difficult in any relationship, but ADHD can easily compound the issues. Their symptoms can leave you feeling disengaged, and your frustration can lead them to feel like a burden. By evaluating how you communicate as a couple, you can discover where communication breakdowns happen. Pay attention to how your spouse receives information. Is it better to write down any requests or errands? Do they focus better when they can have multiple shorter conversations instead of one long one? Ultimately, your marriage and its issues will be completely unique to your situation, so it's important to recognize that your way of solving issues reflects that. When you find what works for you, keep doing that. Check in frequently to ensure that the solution is still working, but stick with it if it is. You will both be much happier and feel more attentive and loving when you find what works.

Chapter Summary

- When communication issues happen in an affected marriage, it can often be due to a disconnect in the way the partners communicate. Symptoms such as short attention spans, trouble with memory and concentration, trouble focusing, and difficulty expressing oneself can lead to both feeling frustrated, angry, and hurt. Discussions lead to arguments which lead to fights, and in the end, no one is happy.

- Some of the most common problems that pop up can be solved by creating rules for engagement—rules that you both stick to when discussing problems. A few examples include eliminating exaggerated statements such as "always" and "never," setting a time limit for the discussion, no name-calling, and making sure you communicate face-to-face, even if you have to use electronic communication.

- When all else fails, it might be time to seek out therapy. Therapy can help you both find ways to open up, manage your underlying issues, and shine a light on the deeper problems in the relationship. Finding the right therapist will help both of you long after you've met your goals as a couple.

In the next chapter, we will talk about common insecurities that crop up in ADHD-affected relationships and how to eliminate those insecurities. We will look at how the disorder can affect self-esteem and self-worth and how to improve those so that feedback feels constructive to both parties.

Day 6

Eliminate Insecurities

Exercise: Find a comfortable position for both of you. Lay down on the bed together, or on a blanket. Breathe in through your nose and out through the mouth. Close your eyes and feel the weight of your body pressing down on you. Move your focus above your head and visualize a stream of warm sunlight flowing down into your bodies and washing away any tension. Imagine it filling up your bodies, from your head all the way down to your toes. The sunlight fills you with a sense of ease.

Imagine the stream traveling slowly up your legs again, into your waist, and then up into your torso. Feel it move through your chest, spreading to your shoulders and back and down into your arms, into your hands and fingers. Let any last areas of tension go as it moves up into your neck and throat. Imagine it moving into your face and up into the very top of your head. Allow yourself to simply sit inside the feelings of warmth, comfort, and calming.

Let go of the image in your own time and open your eyes. Recognize how you felt in that momement and create an intention to carry the awareness into the rest of the day.

In a perfect world, no one would suffer from low self-esteem or poor self-image. Unfortunately, many people in the world do, and this can disproportionately affect those with the disorder. Rates of depression, anxiety, additional disorders such as Oppositional Defiant Disorder (ODD), Obsessive-Compulsive Disorder (OCD), and addictive behaviors appear higher than those with ADHD. They are more prone to serious comorbidities, they also experience higher rates of bullying, ostracization, and difficulty making and keeping friends. These are all tied up together and in the bigger picture, mean that those with the disorder are more likely to internalize conflict and struggle with criticism. This can lead to them checking out of the marriage, too stressed that they don't measure up to some ideal, and deciding not to try instead of constantly feeling as though they are a disappointment.

Additionally, the non-affected spouse feels ignored during conversations and lonely when their partner's hyperfocus pulls them away for long periods of time. You feel as though you constantly have to manage your partner's feelings and avoid things that may cause them to explode. You feel rejected when they make insensitive comments or deeply hurt when they hurl insults specifically designed to target your areas of weakness. You feel as though you are the only dependable one, the only one who can get things done. You start to resent your spouse and feel insecure about the state of your relationship. Finances have you feeling as though you're constantly on the verge of being broke because of your partner's spending habits. You look at your spouse and wonder if they really love you. Do they even care? Are you in this marriage alone? You wonder if they can fall out of love as easily as they seemed to fall in love with you.

"[People with] ADHD labor more than others to define who we are and figure out where we fit. Our brains work faster and that can be exhausting or frustrating. Everyone else has to catch up." (Steed, 2022) You may work extra hard to make people like you, leading you to talk over others, interrupt, or dominate social situations. You relate to other people by sharing your own stories and trying to be the life of the party. You want to be liked, so you come across as charismatic or flirty. When you work so hard to be the center of attention, you come across as self-centered and self-absorbed. Your partner may feel you're not really engaged in the conversation; you're just waiting for a break to one-up their story or get a laugh. They feel you don't really care about what they have to say. Your partner feels like the joy is being sucked from the relationship and their insecurities may get the better of them. You struggle to understand why your partner has doubts about the relationship. The two of you aren't on the same page, and things are deteriorating. What can you do when this happens?

The ADHD brain can often be self-sabotaging, leading to contradictory behavior that doesn't make sense, even to the affected partner. When you don't understand your own brain, you can't communicate what you're thinking or feeling to your partner. Unfortunately, your brain likes to only pick up on criticism. You hear your partner say, "You don't listen to me" and "I'm having doubts about whether or not I really love you." Your instinct is to defend yourself instead of listening to what they're saying to you. This can cause a breakdown in communication. You want to protect yourself from what you see as criticism, so you're ready to lash out and turn the tables.

It also burrows into your brain. You end up hyperfocused on the negatives. When your hyperfocus kicks into overdrive, you end up replaying the negative messages in your brain repeatedly, obsessing about them. You analyze every word and every action to see where you went wrong and how you can fix it. This can kick up your anxiety and depression. You become overwhelmed or numb. Your brain exaggerates the issues or conjures up imagined scenarios. As your brain tries to analyze and fix what's happening, and as you obsess over it more and more, you create your own reality that stands in stark contrast to the truth. Even small things become big problems inside your head. You try to numb the pain by engaging in escapist behavior—whether that's sitting alone playing on your phone for hours, drinking, or making major decisions—such as leaving the country.

You also end up overthinking yourself to the point of destruction. You quit your job because you feel like you're never going to be good enough. You move far away to get a fresh start—only to realize that you desperately miss home. Or, you break up with your partner because you think they deserve better, or that you need to fix yourself before you can be with them. You don't want to get into this mindset because it's self-defeatist thinking. By breaking up or quitting your job, you fulfill the idea that you're not good enough instead of taking responsibility for your mistakes and working towards the clean slate you really want—in the job or relationship. Your problems won't go away if you run away. You're just in a new place with the same problems. Lack of self-love is the root cause of most insecurities. With the way your brain works, you can be your own worst enemy in relationships. You have to learn how to hack your brain and become your own wingman instead.

You don't want to end up in a situation where your insecurities get the better of you. When we let our insecurities drive us, we can end up in situations that crack the foundation of the relationship. Don't let yourself go unchecked with your insecurities. It can push your partner away or tempt you into making terrible decisions that you can never recover from, such as infidelity, crippling debt, addiction issues, or becoming controlling and abusive towards you your partner. This applies to both spouses equally, as the non-affected partner can let their insecurities easily overwhelm them as well. Learn to recognize the signs of insecurity in yourself before they become too much to handle. For example, recognize when you're becoming jealous, angry, self-centered, or argumentative. Your fear will lead to anger, which can lead to hatred, ending with both of you suffering the consequences.

So how do you build confidence in your relationship again? You have to start by building your own self-esteem. There are many ways your brain will try to tell you that you're a bad person, too messed up for love, or that you're not worthy of happiness. Working through those feelings won't be easy. You will always encounter failures in your life. Your mistakes don't define you, though. It's the way you act afterward that counts. Regaining your self-esteem as an adult takes work but will make you feel more secure in yourself, your life, and your purpose. "The core beliefs that shape self-esteem are determined by whether a person appreciates and likes who they are." (Jaksa, 2021) You have to work through the negative self-talk, doubts, and obsessive thoughts before you can get to the place you want to be mentally, where you finally like yourself.

You get into the habit of equating your own mistakes as part of your self-worth while dismissing others' mistakes as simply a mistake. You need to focus on recognizing when negative thoughts appear, challenge those thoughts, and dismiss them. Some people equate their inner voice to someone they don't like or a fictional villain. For example, the unpleasant Professor Dolores Umbridge from *Harry Potter*. They assign a personality to the voice, and it becomes easier to imagine it coming from that person. Professor Umbridge is speaking up, saying "You're worthless, you can't do anything right," and then they can roll their eyes at Umbridge, who is evil and obviously trying to upset them. They take control of their thoughts by understanding that reality is what you make of it. Their thoughts have less power over them. These messages are a kind of cognitive distortion. Your brain wants to view things a certain way to filter out anything that doesn't fit in with that message and dismiss evidence to the contrary.

Another way to stop those negative thoughts in their tracks is to understand and accept your diagnosis. The more you understand what's going on, the more you realize that your negative thoughts are coming from your ADHD. You know that your brain struggles with time management, for example, so if you find yourself running late to important events, instead of beating yourself up, accept that your brain just works differently than others, and you have to manage it differently. It is not a disease; it's a disorder of the brain. It's nothing to be ashamed of or embarrassed by, and you should learn to love who you are, all of you, the ADHD parts included. You should also make an effort to stop comparing yourself to other people. When you compare their best with your worst, you're going to come out looking bad, but it's an inherently flawed train of logic. People only show their highlight reels, the best parts of their lives. You have no idea what goes on behind the scenes in other people's lives.

Instead of focusing on your failures or disappointments, work on identifying and appreciating your accomplishments. Take stock of the things you're proudest of and recognize what that means in the grander scheme. Have you done something unique? Have you gotten an education? Have you created something? Do you have children in your life? You have things about you that are special and worth celebrating. If journaling is something you enjoy, start a gratitude journal that focuses on the things in your life that you're proud of and things that you've accomplished, big or small. Review your journal at the end of every week to see how you've grown and changed. You may be surprised at how much this boosts your self-esteem. You're training your brain to focus on the good instead of filtering it out. Change is easier to see when you can track it.

If you feel like you have a lot of areas where you want to grow, sit down and assess your strengths and weaknesses. Make a list of what you're good at and what you want to improve on. If you want to improve, you have to set realistic and attainable goals. Set goals for the short-term, the medium, and the long-term. Set goals for three months, six months, and one year. Break down your goals into manageable chunks. Then, check in with yourself to make sure that the goals are still attainable and don't beat yourself up if you're not meeting them. It doesn't mean you're a failure; it just means you need to reevaluate your time frame. When you give yourself grace, you may find that you accomplish a lot more than you ever thought you could.

When problems arise in your life, focus on being a problem-solver. You can easily get paralyzed by indecision or feel like you don't know what to do. The secret is, most people don't really know what they're doing—they just get great at winging it. Take charge when you see a problem and ask yourself, "What can I do about it?" Be proactive, and if worst comes to worst, fake it till you make it. If you mess up, oh well, at least you tried. Trying is much better than doing nothing, and you learn something about handling the situation in the future. Don't "should" yourself. Get past the "I could/should/would have done" and tell yourself "I will" and "I can" instead. Putting yourself out there is scary, but you won't know if you can until you attempt to do it. You will also learn more about yourself in the process. It's never too late to learn how to manage and grow with ADHD.

When you're trying to gain self-confidence, you have to ensure you're surrounding yourself with positive people as well. Negative people or relationships will bring you down and make you feel insecure or bad about yourself. You may not notice it right away, but think about the times you've been around people who are constantly complaining to you. You start to complain a lot too, don't you? Or you start to feel angry and upset on their behalf, and then your own life seems unsettled. People who have poor attitudes will bring you down with them. Misery loves company, so to speak. When you are surrounded by positive people, you start to feel better about yourself, your life, and your place in the universe. You can embrace the good and understand that the bad isn't all that bad. By pushing yourself to move away from negative relationships and adopt ones with positive people, you will notice a change in your self-esteem and self-confidence.

Are you being kind to yourself when you make a mistake? Sometimes we want to blame our ADHD or despair that we will never be able to make good decisions because of it. Your disorder can be a challenge for you, but it's not all you are. We often feel as though everyone is judging us for our mistakes or dwelling on the words we spoke, but the reality is, people don't usually remember things like that. You might remember an embarrassing moment at work or cringe when you recall something you said to a friend, but they have likely already forgotten it. You should be kinder to yourself and remind yourself that those little moments will pass from their minds without further thought. You don't need to beat yourself up over it, especially if you own up and take responsibility right away. You forgive other people for minor errors or faults; practice forgiving yourself as well. Being able to forgive yourself will go a long way towards building your confidence back up. You are more than the sum of your mistakes, and you should push yourself to recognize that.

Try to avoid criticizing yourself too harshly in front of others as well. Not only can it reinforce your own negative view of yourself, but it can also make others view you with lower expectations or opinions unfairly. People are most attracted to those with self-confidence. Those who are self-assured are interesting. They present themselves as someone worth knowing. It's tiring to be around someone who always puts themselves down. It's draining. You unintentionally push people away by putting yourself down in front of others. You put out there what you will get back. If you're constantly critiquing yourself and putting yourself down, those attracted to you will draw in people who are just as negative and draining. If you focus on the good things about yourself and bring self-confidence to the table, you'll be able to attract positive people who will, in turn, bring you up as well.

Take small steps forward when you work on your self-image and self-esteem. Of course, you will stumble and make mistakes, and it's tempting to berate yourself, but you need to acknowledge that it's part of the journey; it's part of the learning and growing that you're doing. Track your progress with your therapist or with a journal. Look back every so often to see how you've grown. It might not be obvious in a week, but looking once a month can show you how far you've come. Celebrate your small victories, and revel in your tiny accomplishments. Whatever you need to do to push yourself to recognize the good inside of you. You want to focus on that, not the things that trip you up or make you doubt yourself.

Having positive self-esteem is all about asking yourself two questions: "So what?" and "What's next?" You'll do stupid things, make dumb mistakes, act inappropriately, offend people, or make a fool out of yourself throughout your lifetime. When that happens, you have to stop and ask yourself, So what? What is the big deal? What is the problem? So you accidentally spilled coffee on yourself. So you forgot to turn an assignment in for class? What is the worst that can happen? Seriously, think of the worst things that might happen to you as a result. Let yourself think through the ridiculous scenarios in your head and then ask yourself, "What's next?" How will you deal? How will you fix your mistakes? How will you prevent it so that those dire consequences don't happen? Taking the time to imagine the worst-case can often make you feel better, recognize when you're being silly and when you need to take the proper responsibility. Learning how to separate your silly moments from true moments of growth will help you recognize that there's way more good in you than bad, more positive than negative, and more to like than dislike.

When it comes to working on your self-esteem, your partner should be your ally in this. It's time to examine how you're talking to each other and how you provide feedback. Are you inadvertently tearing each other down? You might be surprised that your actions have an effect on your spouse and on your marriage. Learning how to communicate needs is important but so is learning how to give good feedback. When it comes to providing feedback, are you doing so to encourage your spouse to come to you when they make a mistake or are you making them fear your reaction? Are the two of you able to effectively communicate your needs, or do you place demands on your partner? They should be able to approach you with any problem and feel confident that you will be a safe place for them. If you feel like you're both struggling to be that person, you are contributing to each other's insecurities without realizing it. As a result, you are both unintentionally pushing each other away emotionally.

So how do you start changing things around? You have a new skill to learn—how to be a positive source of feedback for each other. Start by making sure that both of you are actually safe places for the other person to come to. When something goes wrong, make sure that your partner can trust that if they come to you with the problem, you aren't going to berate, belittle, humiliate, or hold it against them at a later point. When you're dealing with a disorder like ADHD, mistakes *will* happen. To ensure that your partner doesn't lie to you or hide their mistakes, you want to be a person that makes them feel that it's okay to make a mistake. Without trust, relationships have no foundation to grow. Establishing that trust is key to ensuring that your partner knows they can talk to you about it if something goes wrong. You also want to ensure that you ask if the issue is one that they need help fixing or if they just want to vent about it. When you push to fix the problem, they might feel resentful or that you don't trust them to fix their own error.

It's also important that you provide a balanced perspective if you have to give your partner feedback. Sometimes it's necessary for the relationship to talk about what is and what isn't working. The ADHD brain wants to take critique as criticism immediately, and it's important to know how to do that. Balancing the positive with the negative is part of that. Let them know the things you see that are good—any growth or positive changes—before diving into whatever issues you might be having. Learning how to balance your perspective is a good way to ensure that your spouse knows you still care, that their mistakes aren't making you lose love for them, and that you're both able to be on the same page through the discussion. Try to ensure that you're not being overly critical either. When you don't know where to draw the line, you can push your partner to the point of anxiety or frustration. They may feel as though they don't know how to make you happy and push you away or no longer make an effort.

When you need to give feedback, make sure you're giving observations and not interpretations. The fastest way to start an argument is to assign meaning to whatever your partner is doing that is bothering you. Instead, pull them to the side and state the observations that you've come across. For example, say "I've noticed that you haven't been telling me about work lately" instead of "You haven't been talking about work lately, I think you're hiding something." The difference is that one is simply an observation, the other is an accusation. Focus on what you need instead of what they're doing wrong. You want them to rise to meet your needs instead of giving up and feeling that nothing they do is right.

Think about how you're going to respond to their reaction. You can control the way you communicate with them, but you can't control how they react to you. Imagine that they get upset; how are you going to respond? If you react with the same level of emotion, you're liable to take a discussion and turn it into an argument or a fight. What you want to do instead is to anticipate how they react and prepare for them. If they get hostile, angry, or defensive, you need to remain calm without being condescending or without infantilizing them. Avoid attacking their character when you're trying to give feedback as well. It's all too easy to fall into the habit of throwing out personal attacks when you're trying to discuss an issue, but the more you do this, the more you're tearing down the person you're supposed to love. Those with the disorder are likely to take personal attacks to heart even more than those unaffected. It can feel like your world is crashing down around you when you hear your partner tell you what you've already been berating yourself about in your head. It gives weight to the harsh words that you already say to yourself.

Your partner might not appreciate what you have to say, so you need to be prepared for them to be unwilling to meet all your expectations. Be willing and ready to compromise. What's the most important thing for you in this issue? How can you adequately achieve that without giving up on your needs? You may have to give up part of your desires to satisfy your partner's own needs. Be prepared to admit when you're wrong too. Sometimes we go into a discussion with all the fire inside, ready to launch a missile at our partner for doing something we don't like or see as wrong. It's entirely possible to be misreading a situation or misunderstanding where your partner is coming from, and this is when you need to serve yourself a slice of humble pie, swallow your pride and admit you were wrong. Your partner will respect you more for admitting that you're wrong.

On the other hand, sometimes, no one is wrong. Sometimes, it's about accepting that your partner is just that way and there's no right or wrong person. For example, if you're constantly upset about your partner leaving their dirty clothes on the floor, you can spend your marriage miserable and berating them for doing it, or you can accept that it's just a part of who they are and that if they haven't changed yet, they aren't likely to change. Letting that go might feel like you're losing at first, but the ultimate win is learning how to make your marriage work. Choosing to accept them doesn't mean defeat. It means that you love them despite their flaws and that you have chosen to pick your battles. This can help your partner feel less insecure because they know that they are loved and that you're both choosing not to sweat the small stuff.

Learning to be more assertive can also help the two of you eliminate those insecurities. Your partner doesn't have to guess when you're open about what you want and how you want it. You can't expect your partner to be a mind-reader. Sometimes we complain that our partners aren't doing things for us, such as making a big deal of our birthdays or buying flowers for us each week, but are we actually communicating that need with them or just expecting that they do it "because?" When it feels like your partner isn't doing what you want, you need to speak up and make sure that you're communicating your needs to them. If you want flowers every week, ask for it. It probably feels as though the spontaneity and romance are lessened by asking, but isn't it better to ask and get what you want than to complain that your partner isn't doing something they have no idea they should be doing?

Similarly to learning how to be more assertive, it's important to learn when and how to say no to your partner. If you frequently take on more of a load than you can handle, and then you find yourself angry at your partner for their insensitivity, the blame falls on you if you haven't mastered the ability to say "no." In an affected marriage, it can be easy to feel as though you *have* to be there for your spouse no matter what, because they can't do it all by themselves. That's both infantilizing and self-sacrificial. You're in a relationship of equals, and you have to learn that saying no can not only ease your burden but empower your spouse as well. They may get complacent with having you do all the things they can't. They may stop trying or growing if they think you'll handle the things they forget about or mess up. The best way to save the relationship from becoming one that is more parent-child is to learn how to say no. Your spouse still needs you in some ways but not in all ways. The two of you just need to decide what is a vital part of helping them cope with their disorder and what is enabling them to learn and growing on their own.

At the end of the day, the two of you are partners, but you need to open up about the things keeping you from becoming closer and making you feel more secure in the relationship. When you share those parts of yourself, you may be surprised at how much the relationship grows and blossoms.

Chapter Summary

- Insecurities in affected relationships are a common result of the disorder's symptoms—both for the affected partner and the non-affected partner. People with the disorder have difficulty navigating social situations, poor understanding of social cues, lack of empathy for others, and take things personally. This can lead to both partners feeling insecure when their needs aren't met.

- Improving self-esteem is one of the best ways to address the insecurities that build up for those with ADHD. Learning how to love yourself, take care of yourself, and see your own self-worth is important to the relationship's health.

- Both of you need to work on how you handle giving and receiving feedback in the relationship. Giving constructive criticism in a way that nurtures a positive relationship is just as important as learning how to accept critique.

In the next chapter, we will go over how to foster more love and empathy in your relationship, and how to grow as a couple.

Day 7

Foster empathy and love

Exercise: Get a pen and paper before you sit down. Sit together in a comfortable place. Do this exercise once every six months or as often as needed. Close your eyes and breathe for a moment until you're both relaxed.

Write down ten ways your partner shows you their love. Share your lists out loud. Next, write down ten more ways your partner has grown in the last six months, then share again. Finally, write down ten things you both want to see in your relationship within the next six months.

When stuck in a cycle of issues with an affected partner, it can feel like there's no getting out. There was a reason the two of you fell in love in the first place. And there is a reason that the two of you have made it work as long as you have. If you two are committed to making it work, you need to get yourself out of your roles. It's way too easy to feel that you, as the non-affected partner, have to step into a parental role to help your spouse. It's easy to feel you'll never get it right, so why bother trying as the affected spouse. If you unintentionally get stuck in those roles, your marriage will suffer. You need to learn how to break free of those roles and find a new normal. It's the only way that the both of you will be able to help grow and nurture the relationship going forward.

Fostering a positive, loving relationship isn't hard, but it might take work, depending on where you two are in the relationship at the moment. If you're feeling distant, it will be harder to get back to where you were before. Mutual trust, respect, and love are the foundations for a healthy relationship. It's a choice that you make each day—a choice to get up and make your partner a priority each and every day. In an affected relationship, it may take extra work on the part of both partners. Affected relationships mean making extra choices and doing extra work for the relationship's health. It can feel like its difficult to muster empathy when you've told your spouse to take the dog out and they have forgotten for the hundredth time. Or when you're struggling to like *yourself* and your spouse is mad because you haven't shown them enough affection.

Empathy is all about putting yourself in each other's shoes and letting yourself see yourself from your partner's perspective. Take an evening and walk each other through a day in the life, being detailed and explaining what tasks you do and how those make you feel. Take turns sharing without interruption. You'll be surprised at what you don't think about that your partner does or the things that you take for granted that your partner works to accomplish. It will open your eyes to the things that the two of you do for each other. When learning how to see life from the other's perspective, it's necessary to understand what you go through day-to-day to understand how you might be adding to the other's emotional burden without realizing it. You want to do this in a way that doesn't promote hostility or anger. This is an exercise all about looking through the other's eyes for a moment.

When working toward fostering a new relationship of love and empathy, you want to encourage change to happen as well. After learning about the other's perspective, commit that you're both going to work on reducing any of the other person's burdens you could inadvertently be causing. Start by asking your partner what you can do during the day, every day, to make them feel cared for and loved. These can be as simple as a request to hold hands while walking together or as helpful as requesting that you take on one chore they hate. Whatever you pick, make sure it's something that they can do reasonably well and doesn't add to their burden in other ways. By making these gestures intentional, you are showing how much you care. It isn't about the gesture itself but the intent behind it. Keep in mind the emotional labor that goes into your gestures. It's nice to be brought fresh flowers, but you add to their labor if you expect that they are the ones who have to cut them down and put them in a vase. Make the gesture thoughtful in a proactive way. If they have to work to enjoy the gift, it's not really a gift.

One simple way to add meaningful empathy and love back into your relationship is to take time out of your schedules to incorporate deeper discussions. Often, we get bogged down by the mundane, day-to-day, and we don't have time for those kinds of discussions. Those affected by the disorder love to share their wealth of knowledge on the topics they're passionate about, and the two of you can really learn from each other when you talk about goals, desires, dreams, interests and even your fears. Find out if their dreams have changed or if they have new dreams. Learn about their desires for the future, what they are currently most interested in, and what they've been learning about. Ensure that your attention is solely focused on the other person when you are having these discussions. They will feel important to you, loved by you, and appreciated when you give them your full attention at such an intimate moment.

The way you respond to them in conversation matters as well. You want to respond to tough things with sympathy and not make it about you, which can be difficult for those with the disorder, as that's how they relate to the world. Instead of saying, "I know how you feel, I went through something just like that," try responding, "That sounds terrible. I went through something similar and felt horrible. How do you feel about it?" You're building empathy for the other person and making it a safe space to share their feelings. You also want to learn to laugh together, at your mistakes, at each other's silly misunderstandings, and occasionally, at the absurdity of life. You have to learn to laugh when things are going wrong, as it's a good way to cope instead of giving in to the feelings of despair and anxiety that can overwhelm you. ADHD can cause you to do some pretty silly or weird things if you think about it. Learning to laugh at your disorder will also help you cope better when it seems to be taking everything to manage it.

When trying to grow the love in your relationship, it's also important to be able to forgive and forget. You will both make mistakes. You will both do things that unintentionally hurt the other person. Holding grudges, holding their past mistakes over their heads, and refusing to forgive will damage the relationship. Being able to forgive can seem easy. You may think you struggle more with being able to forget, but sometimes we say we forgive our partner on the surface even if we haven't really done so deep down. Letting go of the past means letting go. It means not bringing it up again. It means truly being able to move on from whatever your partner did. If you can't do that, you won't have a relationship anymore. It's easy to acknowledge and forgive our own shortcomings as the non-affected partner. We need to extend that same grace to our spouse. You want to treat them the way you want to be treated, which means learning to let go of the hurt. It doesn't have to happen right away, but it's an essential step in learning to grow the love and empathy in your relationship.

Be committed to each other and to your commitment too. ADHD can mean that you're craving new, exciting, and different experiences, and that can lead to destructive behaviors like wandering eyes or, at the worst, cheating. Similarly, as the affected spouse, you may find yourself seeking emotional comfort from another when problems get too hard to handle with your spouse. This is when you need to cling to each other the hardest. You have to be committed harder to the idea of the relationship than you are tempted to stray to reel yourself back. The grass is greenest where you water it, after all.

So how do you get back that spark, that feeling you had when you first met? How do you fall in love with your partner all over again? Experts agree that barring abuse or criminal acts, you can always find your way back into the arms of your partner and fall in love with them again.

Falling in love the first time seemed easy, didn't it? It can be that easy again. You just have to do a little bit of work. Are the two of you actively engaging in time together, apart from responsibilities and children, at least once a month? You need to continue to date each other. Dating is how the two of you connected in the first place. Rekindle the spark with a weekly or bi-monthly date night. You both deserve a break, and you deserve to spend time together. Whether taking a walk together, getting dinner outside the house, or spending a whole weekend away—make each other a priority and make time for each other again. You are supposed to be each other's best friends and it's important that you act like each other's best friends. Build each other up, share important things that happen to you—and be willing to listen—to connect. Connection is a vital part of your marriage. According to research, couples who focus on maintaining their friendship are more likely to be able to move past issues and repair the relationship successfully. When the two of you come up against an obstacle together, treat your partner how you would treat your best friend instead of placing blame or treating your spouse like an infant.

Just as it's good to spend time together, make sure you're also spending time apart. Those with ADHD often need a lot of downtime to recharge and recollect themselves. Even if you're not affected by the disorder, it's still good to have time for yourself and by yourself. It may seem counterintuitive to the relationship—when you're trying to fix what's broken—to spend time apart, but absence does indeed make the heart grow fonder. We find ourselves able to regroup and renew our minds and spirits when we're alone, and it gives us time to miss our spouses as well. We start to see our partners in a more positive light and remember the good in them that we fell in love with in the first place. We have the energy to devote to the relationship when we can rest and recharge. We can deal with issues or problems that arise, give our spouses the attention they deserve, and remind ourselves what it's all about.

You should, of course, have your own hobbies and interests. All healthy individuals should have their own interests outside the mundane and outside of the relationship. Cultivating your own interests is vital for your mental health. However, it's important to do things together as a couple Find a hobby, activity, or sport that the two of you might enjoy together—such as surfing or hiking, taking a pottery or dance class together, or having your own mini book club. Spend time on that hobby together each week too. Read your books, work out or practice to improve. Build each other up too. Sometimes we get down on ourselves about our abilities, especially if we see our spouse doing "better" and may feel discouraged about continuing. Make sure that the two of you are on a team together, not trying to compete. Nothing kills the romance faster than when one spouse makes it into a competition. There is a time and a place for friendly competition but this is about the two of you coming together to spend time together. Additionally, make sure you're going out and trying new things together, too. The ADHD brain craves new, different, and exciting things to keep its dopamine supply going. They want to feel the serotonin flooding their brains. So keep it fed and happy by experiencing new and fun things together. Try adventurous activities like skydiving or more subdued ones like exploring the culinary fare your city offers.

Spontaneity is another good way to keep an ADHD brain engaged. Sometimes we get bogged down by the every day, the mundane, and the day-to-day, and we don't put enough room in the schedule for spontaneous trips to the beach or going camping for the weekend on a moment's notice. It's healthy and good to have a little spontaneity in your lives. It can be simple as well. Getting their favorite candy bar or treat for them when you go to the grocery store or sticking a sweet note in their lunch can go a long way. Romance is all about showing the other person that they care. Love languages are a great way to explore how the other gives and receives their love. Remember to take your results with a grain of salt—but there is still truth to be found in it. Sometimes we receive love differently than we show our love, and it can help to understand your partner's perspective on your kind gestures. It's not that they're ungrateful, but mowing the lawn once a week might not feel as loving to them as spending quality time together or being cuddled in bed at night.

Don't forget to speak like you want to be spoken to. It always feels good to be complimented or praised for something, especially if the one giving it notices a change that you've been working on. Practice what you want by giving your partner those compliments, engaging in meaningful praise that shows you notice and appreciate the changes they've made or how they have grown since you first fell in love. Affirm your relationship by pointing out what you love about your spouse and what you love about the two of you as a couple. Whether that's complimenting how hard they've worked on getting that promotion or affirming how much you love living your best lives with your three cats, it reaffirms that you made the right choices.

There are a lot of ways that couples can reconnect when it comes to intimacy. If you feel as though you're lacking in the bedroom, start with ensuring that your partner's needs are met. For men, they need to feel desired and appreciated. For women, they need to feel valued and emotionally connected. If you're struggling to meet their needs, they may not feel reciprocal desires. It's also important to build intimacy slowly. In order to get that spark back, you need to find what lit the flame to begin with. Then, focus on recreating that initial desire. Fan the flames by moving from there to casual physical intimacy. Light touches, reaching for their hand in public, kisses on the cheek, etc. It's best to keep the contact at the level your partner is comfortable with. Some women find it hard to be physically intimate after the birth of a child, for instance, and often find that their partner trying to initiate contact through random groping can make them feel less desired and less likely to want intimacy. Try asking if you can give them a gentle, slow massage instead. Don't expect it to lead anywhere; you're still building intimacy. Put the work in if you want the results.

When it comes to ADHD, you both might think that having the disorder means learning to live with it, and accept that it comes with plenty to make you annoyed or frustrated. However, the opposite is true as well—there are a lot of qualities that come from ADHD that make for a great spouse. Discover those qualities in your partner and try to work on nurturing them together.

- **Zest for life**. People with ADHD notice so much more than we give them credit for. They notice the little things that we take for granted. They're highly attuned to the world around them. They love to stop and smell the flowers, so to speak. That translates into a huge zest for life and the world around them. They are always finding new ways to appreciate their surroundings or to spruce up their surroundings to bring more joy into your lives. Let them show you how marvelous life can be. Listen when they talk about the wonders they see around them. Hear the passion in their voices as they talk about the things they love. This will give you a new appreciation for life as well.

83

- **Bravery**. When it comes to bullying, people with the disorder understand what it's like more than almost anyone. They understand what it's like to feel different, to be treated poorly for being different, and to feel as though others don't understand and aren't willing to understand you. They are often the ones rooting for the underdog, the ones who champion justice for others. They're willing to stand up and fight for what they believe in. This means that no one will ever treat you badly on their watch. Instead, they will look out for you and encourage you to go after what you want, get the justice you deserve when you're wronged, or fight even when the odds seem insurmountable.

- **Spontaneity**. Those with the disorder make for some of the most spontaneously romantic partners because of the desire to experience new things and the craving to shake up the ordinary. You have a good long-term memory which means that you can surprise your spouse with something they mentioned ages ago. It might be tempting to say "no" when they propose a random, wild and crazy adventure but try to go along with it once in a while because you never know what you might get to experience.

- **Creativity**. People with the disorder see the world from a totally unique perspective. They give something their all when they dive into it and can think of many creative, outside-the-box solutions to problems that surprise us. They are fantastically creative and if you can harness that for a moment, you will come up with ideas that are worth listening to. You can encourage your spouse to pick up a creative hobby or outlet for their ideas and watch them blossom. They can plan amazing parties or trips if given a chance and a little support—giving you experiences you never thought possible!

- **Intelligence**. ADHD doesn't necessarily gift people with higher intelligence, but they can see the world uniquely and think of new ways to solve issues, which gives them an edge when it comes to learning new things. When they hyperfocus, they can pick up new skills in a snap. Think about how smart your spouse is and remind them of that when they have some day-to-day difficulties with organization or forgetfulness. They aren't stupid, they just store memory differently, and their brains want to focus on the most interesting thing at the moment. Pull out the puzzles, board games, or trivia games and watch them work. They will amaze you with their pattern recognition and problem-solving.

- **Parenting skills.** People with the disorder are willing to get down on their children's level, join in on their pretend play, and listen to what their kids have to say. They make great hands-on parents who will provide hours of fun and joy for children. Encourage them when it comes to playtime because they can take something mundane and make it fascinating and interesting to your children. They are naturally good at making kids feel heard as well–they understand what it's like to feel passionate about something important.

- **Sense of humor.** Because of the many ways the disorder can affect their daily lives, they have often learned how to cope using humor. They are often extremely funny and clever and make great jokes when you least expect it. They can help keep you grounded by laughing at how silly life can sometimes be, and they can keep you entertained when your spirits are a bit low. Don't be afraid to laugh with them when they laugh at themselves–it helps you both cope with the way the disorder pops up and reminds you that life is too short to take everything so seriously.

- **Kindness.** People with the disorder have an abundance of compassion and empathy for others. They understand what it's like to struggle, go through difficulties, and feel different in a way that makes them stand out to those who would tear them down for it. They love deeply and are very loyal spouses. Embrace their compassion and find a project that the two of you can get into that helps others–give back to your community or ways that you can help others. The two of you will make an unstoppable team when you work together and use your strengths to balance each other out.

There is nothing better than being married to an ADHD-affected spouse —when you learn to look at the good qualities instead of focusing on how the symptoms affect your life. There are so many ways to learn and grow as a couple when you focus on how having an affected marriage can be a good thing.

For one, it helps you accept and understand that life isn't fair and nobody is perfect. Your spouse may drive you crazy, but they are human, just like you. You can embrace your own imperfections as well. Being with an affected spouse gives you the freedom to give up the notion that you can strive for a kind of perfection within–it doesn't exist and you don't need to stress yourself out trying to achieve it. You and your spouse are unique and you have much to offer the world. Your spouse understands more than anyone what it's like to experience unfairness and they can help you out when things get tough and feel like they aren't going your way. Lean on each other and work through those times together.

You will really learn how to work as a team in an affected marriage. You'll notice that there are some things that your partner manages to execute without issue, and some areas in which they struggle. Divide tasks up by your strengths and weaknesses, and you'll realize that so much more is getting done. It doesn't have to be unequal either. There are ways to make it work that still play to your partner's strength, even if they need more encouragement, help, or reminders to get it done. You can combine chores as well. Maybe doing the dishes isn't their forte, but they can help you dry as you wash. The two of you need to learn to work together to accomplish the things that give you both trouble. Divvying up household responsibilities is another way to work together to divide and conquer. If you're better at remembering the household tasks that need doing and your partner is better at managing the household finances, you be in charge of the master schedule and let your partner take over paying bills and planning out your savings.

Sometimes you'll make a mistake. Your spouse is much more likely to understand that most and is more likely to be willing to forgive–they know how it feels to mess up. The more patient you are with them, the more likely they are also to forgive you when you also mess up or break their trust. You will learn forgiveness and compassion for others when in an affected marriage. You will learn that it's pointless to hold onto grudges and that it's unhelpful to stay angry for small missteps. You also learn patience in an affected marriage. Sometimes it takes a dose of patience to deal with someone with the disorder, and you've learned how to become a more patient person overall. That's never a bad thing. You'll have more patience for your own children and your family, you'll become more understanding of people at work that test you or make mistakes—and it's great that you can understand what it's like to feel for others.

The two of you will become awesome communicators. It's vital to be good at communicating when it comes to the disorder because it can often be in-one-ear-out-the-other, through no fault of your spouse. You will learn how to pick your battles, stop reacting when your spouse's anger or frustration gets the better of them, and pick up on the things they *really* mean when they're struggling to communicate with you. The two of you will learn to stop saying things you don't mean because you know that they are a trigger point for arguments and fights—especially because your partner can misinterpret your words. Good communication can be a game-changer when it comes to the disorder; so you will become great at it, in order to work through the issues that crop up. As a result, you two can navigate any situation, even ones that seem hard or impossible, because of how good you are at working together to overcome.

The two of you can become an unstoppable duo of persevering through the tough times. People with the disorder often refuse to let anything stop them when they get passionate about something, and working together, you become an unshakeable force for good. Your spouse wants to succeed at something when they put their mind to it, and when it comes to your marriage, they will do whatever it takes to succeed. You can weather any storm when you have an ADHD spouse because they won't let something small like a tornado tearing your house apart, or getting fired from your job, stop them from making sure that both of you have a good life. Trust and rely on them when times get hard because with their help you can get through anything.

Fostering love and devotion for each other doesn't have to be hard when you can look at the bright side of your relationship. You are with someone who is unique and brings a unique perspective to the world—one that can bless you both in good times and bad. Learning to embrace the good sides of your spouse while letting go of some of the more frustrating aspects will only help the two of you in the long run. And as an affected partner, you can learn to embrace the crazy, absurd, trying times and help your spouse appreciate the good times all the more.

Chapter Summary

- Learning to empathize with each other will help your marriage succeed. You want to see life from your partner's perspective to understand how it's affecting the other person. Listen to what they have to say, try to understand their point of view, and give them grace and compassion as they give you.

- When things seem hard, stressful, or the disorder appears to be making you struggle with your feelings, try to take time for each other so you can fall in love all over again. Make time to spend together, do something new, be spontaneous, and take time for yourselves in order to let yourself miss them and remember the good.

- There are so many positive aspects to having ADHD that make your marriage wonderful. Your spouse is full of compassion, creativity, kindness, and empathy. They can teach you how to be more patient, persevere through the bad, focus on the good, and let go of the trivial.

Conclusion

ADHD affects marriage in numerous ways. It can be difficult to deal with a spouse that has the disorder. Symptoms like trouble paying attention, impulsivity, forgetfulness, emotional dysregulation, difficulty in maintaining relationships, poor organizational skills, difficulty understanding and empathizing with others, and more can affect how the two of you interact and function. You feel as though you're at your wit's end sometimes, and you often feel as though you've taken on a role as more of a parent to your partner than an equal. This can take a toll on your feelings for your partner and can leave you feeling as though you're ready to cut your losses. It's not only on the affected partner, though. The non-affected partner may be contributing by nagging, getting angry or frustrated, infantilizing their partner, berating them, or making them feel guilty or unappreciated.

It doesn't have to be like that, though. The two of you need to understand more about the disorder in order to tackle how to improve it. Studying up on the disorder will help, as will the both of you acknowledging that there is a problem and that problem is affecting the relationship. It's important to recognize the way your disorder is making your partner feel, and it's important that as the non-affected partner, you're acknowledging how your criticism and nagging are making them feel. Start by separating who your partner is from their symptoms. Recognize that they aren't their disorder, that it's a part of them but not the sum of their whole.

Some of the most common relationship problems with ADHD can be solved by learning to work with the disorder instead of against it. Sometimes we want our spouse to just "be normal," but there is no normal with the disorder. You need to put strategies in place to help each other through the problems. Learning how to navigate the disorder will involve becoming more educated about it and figuring out, through trial and error, how to manage the symptoms. You need to put a plan in place to help with navigating chores and household duties and figure out the best strategies to help navigate social situations and understand each other better. Having empathy for the things that your partner goes through as the two of you navigate the symptoms will help you both understand each other better and be more loving and forgiving when things aren't going the way you want or when the disorder is making it difficult to communicate.

Learning how to understand nonverbal cues is one of the best ways that people with the disorder can understand their partner better, especially when we express ourselves a lot through nonverbal means. The two of you can work together to navigate social situations, leading to less frustration, less miscommunication, and less misunderstandings. Having a plan going in will minimize the amount of social blunders that crop up and help your spouse recognize when they're doing things like dominating the conversation or they need some time to recharge. People with the disorder often take criticism and bad experiences to heart, so it's important to be kind when you point out what you want to help your significant other overcome. Conflict will arise, and it's important you know how to navigate it properly. When it comes to discussing sources of conflict, try to be understanding and sympathetic and clear and concise. Your partner will feel shame and embarrassment and may lash out to hide their feelings, but understanding will go a long way towards helping the both of you navigate communication issues.

When your partner feels good about themselves and good about their relationship with you, they're more likely to be open to hearing feedback. Working on your sense of self-identity, separating it from your ADHD, can help you improve self-esteem, which will give you the opportunity to feel secure enough to grow in the relationship. As the non-affected spouse, learning to stand up for yourself and how to say "no" is just as important as gaining self-esteem is to the affected partner. You want to strive for a point where you can put yourself first while still being a considerate partner to your spouse. The goal is to give them a hand while also letting them be independent and feel as though they are your equal.

Though it will be difficult, it will be worth it when you start to see the relationship changes that you've been looking for. You may not know it, but the two of you are starting a very important journey together. You are learning how to accept each other, flaws and all, and how to work together to become a better couple and better friends. Being friends first should be the goal. Treat each other as you would treat your friends and treat each other as you want to be treated. Compliment them when they've done something you appreciate, and make them feel respected, heard, and appreciated. Remember that having the disorder isn't all bad, either. Having ADHD gives people a greater sense of compassion, stronger loyalty, more creativity, and better problem-solving skills. These, when put into effect, can make your spouse into a super-powered spouse, friend, and parent.

It will take more than seven days of work to get there, but using the tips, tricks, and techniques in this book will start your new journey together on the right foot. You have the opportunity to take a good relationship and make it a great one. Don't be scared to talk to each other, lay out what you need going forward, and work together to make that happen. Stumbling blocks will come up, and mistakes will be made along the way, but the two of you are empowered now to make the future exactly how you want it to be.

If you liked this book and found it helpful, please leave a review on Amazon.

Printed in Great Britain
by Amazon

86103895R00061